LOOKING BACK ON
GOD'S HAND IN MY LIFE

D1649150

Beams of
HEAVEN
Guiding Me

ROY ADAMS

DENVER, COLORADO

Outskirts Press, Inc.
http://www.outskirtspress.com

ISBN: 978-1-4787-3837-4

Library of Congress Control Number: 2014912758

Outskirts Press and the "OP" logo are trademarks belonging to Outskirts Press, Inc.

PRINTED IN THE UNITED STATES OF AMERICA

Contents

Preface

I like to hear people tell their stories. I like to read about their journey. I perk up when I sense a personal narrative about to begin. I'm curious to know where someone's coming from; what happened; how things came down for them. And I notice that, however similar, each account contains its own special twists, distinguishing it from all the others—much like a fingerprint sets us apart.

That last point about fingerprints, notwithstanding, I felt compelled at the outset of writing my own story to put these candid questions to myself: With millions of other stories already on the "market," does the world really need one more? Will yours contain any ingredient not already found in the existing global pool?

Eventually, I answered those questions with a yes. To have said no would have been ungrateful. When Jesus admonished the restored demoniac to go home to his friends, "and tell them what great things the Lord has done for you" (Mark 5:19, NKJV),* it was not as if Jesus meant to suggest there were no other similar stories already out there. Rather, He knew that this man's narrative, in critical ways unique to him, would make a difference in the telling. In the same vein, long before the demoniac's time, Nebuchadnezzar had been inspired to tell his harrowing story for his own generation and those that would come after. He wanted "the peoples, nations and men of every language who live in all the world" to know about "the miraculous signs and wonders that the Most High God has performed for me" (Dan 4:1, 2).

My own experience falls far short in both gravity and drama, compared to those two biblical examples. But it's against that background, nevertheless, that I share these memories. I want to join Nebuchadnezzar in telling about God's "miraculous signs and wonders" in my life. And I want to say with the ancient psalmist (from a passage that probably motivated Jesus' instructions to the demoniac): "Come and listen, all you who fear God; let me tell you what he has done for me" (Psa. 66:16).

This is not, strictly speaking, an autobiography; nor is it, strictly speaking, a memoir. Rather, it's a hybrid, a cross between the two, leaning a tad more heavily, however, in the direction of memoir. So I call it that. Selected chapters of my journey thus far, it comes with the hope that the events and experiences described might prove useful to readers, especially younger readers with their entire lives still before them. Their journey will never parallel mine exactly, but if mine can somehow nudge them to press ahead when they otherwise would have thrown in the towel, then this humble effort will not have been in vain.

All biblical references in this work, unless otherwise indicated, are from the New International Version Classic Reference Bible, copyright 1988 (Zondervan).

PART I

There is a tide in the affairs of men,
Which, taken at the flood, leads on to fortune;
Omitted, all the voyage of their life
Is bound in shallows and in miseries.
On such a full sea are we now afloat;
And we must take the current when it serves,
Or lose our ventures.
—*Julius Caesar*, Act 4, scene 3, 218–224

Those who go down to the sea in ships,
Who do business on great waters,
They see the works of the Lord,
And His wonders in the deep.
Psalm 107:23, 24 (NKJV)

When the Letterhead Is Gone

"Roy Adams!"

I'd just been introduced to Ezra Faider, a General Conference (GC) auditor, who'd recently arrived on the campus of the University of the Southern Caribbean in Maracas, Trinidad, for a scheduled financial audit. In the company of an assistant, he was sitting in front of his computer in the living room of the university's guest house where he was housed, and where I also would be staying during my visit for a speaking appointment.

Didn't write down his exact words, but I think I'm reproducing their substance fairly accurately here.

"I've been following your writings over the years," he continued, "and I think your editorial 'When the Letterhead Is Gone' is the best article on leadership I've ever read. I hand out copies of it at auditing workshops I conduct."

I don't think it showed on my face, but I was stunned. After all, my encounter with him was taking place in October of 2013, and the editorial he referred to was published in *Adventist Review,* April 25, 1996—more than 17 years earlier! In complimenting me on the piece, he'd joined a chorus of several others who'd spoken or written to me about it in the period immediately following its publication. But Faider's memory of the article after 17 years astounded me.

I myself had never forgotten the editorial, of course—and, indeed, I've had many occasions to reflect on its message since my own retirement in November 2010. But Faider's unexpected reference to it led me to go back and actually re-read what I'd said. And I came away with the feeling that perhaps nothing else I've written expresses more succinctly my whole philosophy of Christian ministry.

That being the case, and considering the nature of some of the issues I'll be discussing in this memoir, I thought it fitting to reproduce it here, for the benefit of those who never saw it in the first place, or who've long since forgotten it. Here it is (in italics)—all but its final paragraph:

The letter arrived on my desk. Three quarters of a page. Typewritten. Every word bespoke the need for a new typewriter ribbon. I glanced at the signature. I recognized the name.

The writer, in his heyday, had the authority to command the services of a dozen secretaries with computers. His messages went out on official stationary, unnerving subordinates and bringing hope to nervous prospects looking for a job. Now as I stared at the sheet of plain bond paper lying on my desk, one compelling detail struck me: the letterhead was gone!

For me, a good letterhead carries with it the aura of prestige, suggesting that the person using it is no fly-by-night operative acting on his or her own, but rather is backed up by corporate power, by institutional clout. And it was against this background that I studied the letter lying on my desk. Its author, now retired, and with no access to a single secretary, had been left to hunt and peck his way across the keyboard of a Smith-Corona, eraser and liquid paper at the ready.

It gave me pause. And I drew three lessons:

1. Our tenure in whatever office or position we hold within the church is temporary*. It does not last forever. And it might just be that someone whom we least expect will someday be sitting right where we are today. 'I have to be careful how I treat you fellas,' the pastor with whom I interned years ago used to say, 'because you'll be deciding my sustentation one day,' How easy it is for the present occupants of position and power to forget that!*

There is no room for arrogance, no room for lording it over those we regard as our subordinates. People are not mere objects to be pushed around, like pawns in a game of chess. We should cultivate a gentle sensitivity in the way we handle people—even those to whom we owe nothing and from whom we expect nothing.

2. We do not know today whose help we'll need tomorrow. In the days when the man in my story appeared larger than life to me, I would never have imagined—in my wildest dreams—that he'd one day be sitting across the table from me, so to speak. Yet here he was asking whether we would accept his article for publication in the Review. And it fell to me to decide.

I pondered the amazing development and reminded myself that one day, should time last, I too might be bringing a similar request to the future occupant of that same chair—someone who's probably right now attending college (or even academy!)

That's how life is. What goes around comes around. Roles change. And none of us is in for life. We serve at the pleasure of the church. And those who at any given moment find themselves in a position to determine the job security of another ought always to remember that their own time is coming. We who wield power and influence within the church should pay attention to that all-important sign along the career pathway: "Proceed with caution—tables turning."

The one quality that softens the shock of this kind of change is humility. The man in my story was highly placed, but I remember him as a humble person. So now, with the letterhead gone, he could continue to be the same self-effacing person he'd always been.

3. We need to be sure of our essential identity. When all the artificial trappings of officialdom have been removed from us, who are we? The man in my story had retired. And, however unfortunate, there are few things in the Adventist Church that can cause people to see themselves as irrelevant more quickly than retirement. This can spell disaster to those who, over a lifetime, have experienced their identity solely in the context of position and power.

I thanked Faider for his kind compliment; and I think he knew what I meant when I said: "I'm right there now."

Of course, I was never involved in the high trappings of position and power within the church. Still, getting to the level of the GC (as I did) does bring with it—if you don't misunderstand me—a certain measure of clout. There is, unfortunately, a pecking order inside the church—spoken or unspoken; and once having experienced it from the "upper floor," you miss it (or at least notice it) when it's gone. My telephone still rings, but most of the time, it's from telemarketers trying to foist their wares on me. And for the calls I take, I miss having an assistant to screen and handle them. At the office, when my computer would break down or malfunction, my assistant would simply call "the IT guys," and they'd come by and put me back on track.

Now, all that has changed. There was a brief cushion period just after leaving the office, a time when I received some transitional help. But without being expressly told, I knew that that grace period had come to an end when my calls for the most minimal help went unheeded, and I was left high and dry with a malfunctioning machine on my desk. (Many times I've had to press my son Dwayne—a self-taught computer whiz—into service. He lives in another city far away, but he's always been so willing, and would vociferously protest if I so much as hinted I was taking too much of his time. Even so, I've learned to solve a surprising number of issues on my own, necessity being the eternal mother of invention.)

I know the letterhead is gone when new acquaintances ask for my business card, and I have none to give. I know the letterhead is gone when I sign important emails with the simple words "Roy Adams," unembellished by any accompanying title. I know the letterhead is gone when Spring Meetings, Annual Councils, and North American Division Yearend meetings come and go without a single change in my schedule. I know the letterhead is gone by the sense I get of being totally shut out of the important administrative functions and happenings in the church; from the feeling of being completely irrelevant to the entire process; from the sense of "not being needed." Like the so-called "non-essential workers" during a major storm, I get to stay home.

And I'm loving every minute of it!

Not that I have yet experienced the luxury of being "idle." In fact, to quote a common saying, "I have so much to do I don't know how I ever found time to go to work." It's perhaps one of the biggest surprises for me in retirement—how much there still is to do; how full my daily schedule still is; how little time I've had thus far for the rocking chair.

Nor can I adequately explain what keeps me so occupied. All I know is that my to-do list is just as long as when I was in active service for the church. The speaking appointments are still there—though not as frequent or as heavy as before. (In my first overseas appointment following retirement—to New Zealand in January 2011—I spoke some 14 times for camp meeting; and I vowed to myself that that would be my last engagement with such heavy lifting.) It helps that I don't receive as many invitations as before. The reality is that not having any longer a GC budget to travel on, I've suddenly become exponentially more expensive to invite, since my hosts must now foot the entire bill.

Working at the GC for all those years got to me more than I'd realized. The camaraderie, the deadlines, the travel, the ceaseless activity—it all unconsciously embedded itself into my psyche. While at my post, I hardly ever had any nighttime dreams about the place. But since my retirement, I've dreamed about the GC, the *Adventist Review*, or some aspect of the two, numerous times, with a variety of different takes: I'm still working there; I have a new office down the hall; the entire office area is being renovated, and I'm struggling to find my new location; I'm heading to one of the many meetings in the complex; my wife and I are attending a GC session and wondering how it is that we're able to pick and choose end-row seats up in the stands, with Brian Williams of NBC news sitting behind us with his family; and on and on.

Inconsequential to be sure—even nonsensical at times; but it all

probably showed how psychologically married to my work I'd become; and how intertwined my whole psyche had grown to the place
and people, built up over the course of more than two decades. Or
perhaps it reflected in some confused way the pain, as you will see,
that characterized the closing period of my work at the headquarters
complex.

Retirement brings with it a certain measure of freedom. Apart
from the unending chores in and around the house, the things I now
do are *what I want to do*. You couldn't pay me to go back to regular
work in an office; to go back to reading term papers, correcting exams, evaluating manuscripts, editing and re-editing articles, attending
endless committee meetings, etcetera, etcetera. I'm so finished with
all those workshops and planning days and envisioning events (to
come up with all those meaningless goals and mission statements).

In the fall of 2013 I remember looking over the schedule for a professional meeting I used to attend. As I read the arcane descriptions
of the various presentations, I was like "been-there-done-that"—to
put it in the vernacular of today's younger set. And it surprised me
how jaded I'd become. Not, I believe, out of tiredness or disengage-
ment; but, rather, as if from a new perspective of what's important and
what's simply playing to the gallery; spinning wheels for the sake of it;
going round and round the mulberry bush for no good reason. I felt
so done-with-all-that!

That same retirement jadedness (if I may call it that) extends to
some things going on in Adventist officialdom, as well. The massive
"study" (as I write) on the role of women in the church, for example.
My response tends to be: Enough already! The hour is so late, the issues out there so huge, the spiritual and moral confusion in society
so widespread and complex, why spend time, effort, and money on a
thing like that! After all, it's not as if we're dealing with some new issue. No, we've plowed these grounds before—by some estimates, for
as much as 60 years! And what women in the church are seeking is
simply a chance to participate in the preaching ministry of the church
and, like their male counterparts, be formally recognized for it. That's

all they want—full participation in the mission of the church.

So perhaps the Lord retired me just in time. I'd have found it too difficult (forgive me) to deal with such needless squander of resources and time. And on those days when I'm tempted to fuss about what's going on, I remind myself that for me the letterhead is gone—to the extent it was ever there; that others now occupy the desks where once I sat; and that ultimately everything—the church itself included —lies in God's mighty hands.

I've personally felt those powerful hands at work in my own life and ministry. God has been my strong tower, my guiding light. And that's what this memoir is all about.

CHAPTER 1

My Earliest Memories—They Feel Like 200 Years Ago

IT SURPRISED ME that the story—tragic as it was—brought a chuckle.

It was December 2011, and the campus of Virginia Polytechnic Institute in Blacksburg, Virginia (site of a massacre by a lone gunman only four and a half years earlier) saw yet another tragic shooting. In the wake of the latest incident, one news report said, campus officials had decided to step up security across the school's entire 4-square-mile property.

I suspect most people listening to the same report would have focused on the tragedy itself and on the resulting security beef-up. I did that too. But one other detail also caught my notice and brought the chuckle just mentioned. It was the size of the campus: *four square miles*. I found it funny to think that the West Indian island of Carriacou where I was born is only nine square miles bigger than the Virginia Tech campus!

My earliest childhood memories in this tiny place (a parish of Grenada) seem so utterly misty that I sometimes think they happened 200 years ago or more. Memories of Six Roads, the village where I was born and the first place I ever knew, getting its name from the six roads that branch off from its main intersection. Memories of near total darkness in the village after sundown in those days before electricity came. And in connection with that darkness, memories of my superstitious childhood fears of danger lurking all along those country roads—not of bandits or of robbers (there was none of that), but of zombies and spirits. Certain large trees were considered particularly haunted, the older folks regaling us young tots with tales of huge, oversized dogs and other four-legged creatures seen near them in the dead of night; tales of immaculately-dressed strangers strolling at the crossroads at midnight in the moonlight.

I remember hearing stories of witches (strangely, not of wizards) who turned vampire in the night, sucking blood from village people sleeping in their beds; and I remember what we did as boys returning from school, when we approached someone rumored to be a witch. Mischievously, we'd walk on both sides of the road, forcing the suspected (and un-amused) sorcerer to walk between us. Switching sides after passing them, we would consider ourselves to have "tied them up," so they couldn't do their bloody work that night.

I remember little babies, especially those deemed attractive, being outfitted with amulets (good luck charms)—little pouches filled with garlic, herbs, powders, and other substances, worn under the clothes for protection against spirits, spells, and the evil tongue of jealous people in the community.

When someone died—not a frequent occurrence on a small island of 10,000 people—a village crier (always a man) would walk through the surrounding areas blowing a conch shell to gain attention. Then speaking in English, broken English, and patois, he would announce the name of the deceased, give the day and time of the funeral, and finish the solemn tidings with an open invitation to the burial ceremony and related activities: "Come one, come all!" he'd say before signing off.

Following such announcements, elders in the village sometimes would tell how they'd seen the dead person's spirit "traveling" days or hours before they died. Sometimes as the older folks gathered at nightfall to visit, the conversation would turn to zombies and spirits. And as much as they scared the daylight out of us, we kids couldn't get enough. We'd listen to hair-raising tales of all sorts of things that go bump in the night. Not infrequently, big sister would choose that very time to discover that a certain little tyke had not yet washed his feet for the night, and should go outside or around the house to do it. Frightening stuff, with every movement of every leaf or straw bringing sheer dread!

This lurking fear, notwithstanding, it was a care-free childhood that I remember, running around the village (when I was very small) in shirt tails; chasing what we called "rollers" down the hill; searching through the neighborhood in the early morning hours (especially after the family had moved to the village of Brunswick, a mile or so away) for ripe mangoes that had fallen during the night from our neighbor's trees or ours; hunting waterfowl in the mangroves across the cow pastures, catching one or two, and having a cookout with my cousins and friends; joining my big brothers and cousins as they hunted manicous (opossums) on moonlit nights, with dogs specially trained for the purpose; accompanying them as they tended the animals in the lime-fields of a semi-public local estate in the early hours of the morning before daylight; or swimming far out to sea with them and their friends on Sunday mornings.

One of the aims of those Sunday morning ventures was to acquire bragging rights for going further out to sea than any other group of boys. And you judged that by how high or low were the houses in the village that you were able to see above the trees that lined the beach. It wasn't a big deal to see Cousin Toppin's house high up on the hillside. But if you were able to spot Uncle Victor's house sitting on a much lower elevation, then that would mean you'd gone a mile or more further out to sea. Just a kid, I remember having to touch the back of my older brother Dennis for support during those Sunday morning expeditions, feeling safe on the way out (since I was behind, so to speak), but petrified on the way in (since I was also behind), my mind conjuring up all kinds of frightening creatures moving in to take a bite or even pull me off my brother's back. (I'm still mystified that we took such dangerous chances, that no one ever drowned, and that we never ran into sharks or other dangerous marine predators.)

As a boy, I couldn't get enough of the sea, and always looked forward to the beach-side picnic the first of August every year, when scores of people in the village and beyond came out for the all-day swimming party. It was during one of those events that I kicked against a rock while trying to swim in shallow waters, and hurt my big toe—a hurt I sometimes feel still today.

A story of my boyhood that I've told several times before (including in an article for *Ministry* magazine some years back) bears repeating here. It comes from those teen-age years when girls are uppermost in the heads of young boys. In my case, those were also the days when we young men had something bordering on fear (if not dread) for those mysterious creatures we called the opposite sex.

And so, with a dance party coming up, some of us, boys, would want to know ahead of time whether that certain young woman we'd been drooling over would accept our offer for a dance after we'd crossed the entire hall to ask her hand. We knew it would be most embarrassing to have to head back to the boy's side empty-handed, all eyes on us. So we wanted to know the outcome in advance.

To find out, we'd take the large (big-headed) main key to the house and place it in the family Bible at a particular chapter (that I will not identify), strapping the Bible tight around it. Then two of us boys, the tips of our fingers at the neck of the key-head, would hold the suspended Bible in the middle. The contraption in place, we'd both repeat a formula (that I will not mention); then we'd each, in turn, put our question. My friend might say: "Will Susan dance with me Friday night if I ask her?"

If the answer was no, the Bible would remain stationary between our fingers; but if the answer was yes, the Bible would turn of its own accord and drop to the floor, unless we grabbed it first.

The uncanny phenomenon impressed me that the Bible was not an ordinary book. But it also served to strengthen the force of a widespread belief in the community that the Bible was a dangerous book, not something to dabble in. Rumor had it that some who'd delved into certain forbidden portions of the mysterious book had ended up crazy or unstable. It would take a while for the Lord to rid me of all these morbid fears and borderline spiritualistic practices.

My earliest boyhood years were steeped in poverty. We were not the poorest family around, but we *were* poor. As a small boy, I remember six siblings—Nathaniel, Dennis, Maudlyn, Husford, Flossie, and Claradell. My oldest brother George (now deceased) had probably already left home before I was old enough to pay attention. I remember him only later when he came back from Florida (where, with many other young men from the islands, he'd been recruited to help with the citrus harvest). That's when, as a prank, my oldest sister Maudlyn made me sweep the public dirt road that led down to our house, just because George had just arrived back on the island and was headed home. (And I was glad to do it. After all, my big brother was coming!)

Our father, an expert carpenter, was away during all of my younger years, working in places like Trinidad, Venezuela, and finally Aruba (with the Lago Oil and Transport Company). I remember that from Aruba, he would send home to our mother the grand sum of $40.00 every three months for all the family needs. How our mother ever managed on that meager allowance I will never know. But if I heard her say it once, I heard her repeat a hundred times her favorite line when the food supply in the house was running low: "The Lord will provide." She did not frequent church every Sunday, but she was a very spiritual and godly person.

Fortunately, like most families on the island—once we moved to Brunswick—we lived in our own house, on our own property, with no one at our door collecting rent or mortgage at the end of the month, And this one factor made a world of difference. In regard to crops, we grew on our own land the three mainstays of the island: corn, peas, and cotton. It was no fun picking and bagging cotton; but the furry commodity brought in much needed funds when sold to the government each year. The government would buy it from us at some predetermined price, then give us a bonus at Christmas time, if sales went well. (Our mother looked forward to those Christmas bonuses!)

As for the corn and peas, they were supplemented by other food crops, such as sweet potatoes, cassava, okra, peanuts ("groundnuts" we called them), and several others. And from time to time, we had fish, caught fresh by local fishermen in the tropical waters surrounding the island. Other times we had (imported) salted codfish ("salt fish" we called it). In addition there were the typical tropical fruits in season—papayas, mangoes, sugar-apples, guavas, oranges, etc.

As kids, we came home from school at the end of a typical day to a meal of coo-coo and callaloo—the coo-coo, made from corn (ground laboriously in our own hand-operated mill), mixed with water, a little shortening, and a sprinkling of salt. The callaloo was a side dish made from okra or dasheen leaves, sometimes mixed with salt fish. In the morning for breakfast we added water and fresh cow's milk (when available) to the left-over coo-coo to make what we called coo-coo tea. Most days, if we kids took anything for lunch at school, it was parched or roasted corn; then to complete the monotonous cycle, we came home again to coo-coo and callaloo for the evening meal. (Today, whenever I see coo-coo on any menu, I know it doesn't have my name on it; I've already had my life-time share!) After the pigeon peas were harvested, dumpling and peas (with coconut) became the looked-forward-to favorite meal, interrupting the coo-coo and callaloo routine. And those Sundays when we had chicken and rice were like heaven itself!

Once a year all of us, children, went through a scheduled purging, which the older folks saw as a necessity. You gulped down a tablespoonful of hellish-tasting castor oil, in a glass of ginger ale to keep you from actually vomiting back the stuff. The unpleasant aftereffects of the concoction goes without saying, especially with only outdoor toilets in those days; but our mother did something that almost made us look forward to the miserable experience. We were not to eat anything heavy; but without fail, she would kill one of the chickens from our own yard, and later in the day prepare the most delicious chicken soup you can imagine—with small dumplings in it!

Um-um good!

With no clocks in the house, we timed our departure for school by how far the sun had risen over the Mount Royal hills, then took off in bare feet for the 2-mile trek to Hillsborough Government School, in those days a generally open, breezy place, where the singing of the morning marching song following assembly struck fear into my bones, anticipating (most times unnecessarily) the unpleasantness and calamities the day might hold for me.

I was not a bad student, and I liked my teachers. Frequently finding myself at or near the top of the class, I would receive from my mother the most appropriate compliment I've ever heard any parent give, at precisely the correct calibration. Sometimes I'd overhear her talking to a visitor to our home about my accomplishments in school—not in a boastful manner, but with deep motherly pride and a sense of anticipation as to what this boy was going to become. I'm sure she never read a book on parenting, but she had every maternal instinct right. With only a third grade education herself, she was my first inspiration in life and a catalyst to all my educational pursuits.

I fault her on just one thing. The school being a good walking distance away, she kept my little sister and me home on Fridays, believing that four days a week was enough for us at that tender age. Which probably explains my lifelong struggle with math. Friday, for some reason, was the day when new math concepts were introduced. I knew how to add. But missing Fridays meant being absent for those introductory classes in subtraction. And what a predicament that landed me in come Monday and the rest the week with my class exercises! I would add left to right, right to left, up and down and diagonally, but always I would get the answers wrong. I can't remember when I finally got subtraction, but I now know that 5 minus 3 is 2—and not 8.

But my mother meant well. And I tell people that in spite of the poverty, the privations, and the obvious disadvantages of my early years growing up, if I had to do it all over again—given what I know now—I'd go right back there and be born, provided I get to have the same mother. For those early experiences have shaped me, and given me an outlook on life that I would never exchange for that of those born to privilege.

We were Anglicans when I was growing up. Not staunch—we were absent from church most Sundays. But Christmas and Easter (especially Easter) were sure to find us in the pews. Some of the powerful Easter hymns linger in memory, and I can still hear the congregation singing in the predawn hours of an Easter Sunday that great 17th century hymn:

> Alleluia! Alleluia! Alleluia!
> The strife is o'er, the battle done;
> Now is the Victor's triumph won;
> O let the song of praise be sung.
> Alleluia!"

And I particularly liked the triumphant words of the second stanza:

> "Death's mightiest powers have done their worst,
> And Jesus hath his foes dispersed;
> Let shouts of praise and joy outburst.
> Alleluia!"

In comparison with the services at the Catholic Church on the other end of town, the Anglican worship was bland. It did not have the eye-catching "bells and whistles" that attracted me to the Catholic Church. Besides, my boyhood crush was Catholic. But I took comfort in the fact that as Anglicans we had the Queen of England on our side. That ought to count for something, I frequently told myself.

There were other denominations on the island, of course—some of them fly-by-night, their itinerant preachers lighting up the evening darkness of the village from time to time with kerosene lanterns, as they vied for new converts from the members of the two mainline churches. As professor Haddon Robinson says somewhere, "Not much happens in a small community. [So] villagers take their excitement wherever they can find it."

And that's what happened in our case. Without the distraction of radio or television in those days, one or more members of my family sometimes would gravitate toward one of these open air evening events for shorter or longer periods, joining the ever-changing roadside audience to listen to the preaching. The preacher (male or female) was usually accompanied by a small group of their members to lead out in the music. The singing was usually a cappella, but sometimes the groups came with musical instruments. It all provided free entertainment to an otherwise dull evening—something to do; somewhere to go. But however earnest the preachers, they didn't faze the Adams family. *No, we were Anglicans!*

And of all the groups we considered Johnnies-come-lately, Seventh-day Adventists were the most despised—so much so that at home among ourselves we called them "Seven Devils." I remember the day a group of them came to our place for (what they called) their "field day." When, after making it clear we didn't want their tracts, they proceeded to leave them anyway, one of my sisters threw the leaflets back at them.

Then came Hurricane Janet—September 27, 1955. The storm left mountains of destruction in its wake, and proved a turning point in my life and that of several members of my family.

Among the buildings badly damaged was the (only) Adventist church on the island. Windows blew out and several parts of the structure fell, killing, incidentally, a young Adventist woman who, with her family, had fled to the place for safety. With their church now out of commission, the Adventists transferred the evangelistic meetings they'd been holding there to a tent hastily set up in a public recreation area.

No member of the Adams family ever would have darkened the doors of an Adventist church in those days. And at any rate, we had no idea those meetings were taking place. But the tent on familiar public property caught our attention; and, given the neutral setting, my sister Flossie and I decided to check it out. (Incidentally, it was Flossie who'd thrown the tracks back at the Adventists the day they came to our place.)

The young evangelist was a small man, but seemed to grow larger as he spoke. We'd never heard such things before. As Adventists, we sometimes repeat the same stuff over and over again to ourselves, until we're bored with it. Meanwhile, multitudes wait in ignorance, hungry to hear the message we so often take for granted. Following each meeting, we'd go home and talk about what we'd learned. Indeed, we got so engrossed in the meetings that when they transferred them back to their (now-repaired) church, we found ourselves (surprise, surprise!) willingly setting foot into the once-forbidden place. In the end, both Flossie and our oldest sister Maudlyn were baptized (the same day) by Pastor Henry Gabriel, the minister who'd taken over after the young evangelist left.

Shortly thereafter, joining a wave of other Caribbean immigrants, Flossie (too new to Adventism to have heard anything about "being unequally yoked") left for the UK, to marry her Roman Catholic fiancé. In time, as it turned out, her husband Simon would himself become a staunch Seventh-day Adventist. And so would my mother, another sister (Claradell), and a cousin (Jacob). Flossie and her husband (now deceased) would later move to Toronto (Canada), where she would become an elder in her local church; her two daughters, Margaret and Jean, would shoulder heavy responsibilities in the same church, including serving as elders; and her only son Frankie would become an Adventist pastor and conference youth director. (He remains active in ministry today in Ontario.) I'm still dumbfounded that God was able to get members of the Adams tribe to join a church they once despised with such passion.

But God had a somewhat tougher time with me than with the others. For however impressed I was by those evangelistic meetings my sister and I attended, I did not quickly join the church. That would come in a manner that only God could plan. And today I look back with sheer wonder at the way He eventually led me to final conviction and surrender; the gentle tactics He employed to prod this defiant soul to even enter the Adventist ministry; His miraculous leading as, dirt-poor, I launched out into the unknown in search of higher education; and His gracious providences in my life through the decades. The Israelites in their journey were led by a visible pillar of cloud and fire. I, for my part, would sense—again and again—the presence of invisible beams of light from heaven, an invisible hand guiding.

And that's what I come to now.

CHAPTER **2**

On to the GBSS... and into God's Opening Providence

AS WE WERE attending those evangelistic meetings, I'd already applied for admission to the Grenada Boys' Secondary School (GBSS), in my time the most prestigious school in the country, taking students from what in the United States would be considered high school through college. Located in St. George's, the nation's capital, it boasted students and faculty from all over the island and beyond. To be accepted as a student was a plum; and sometime during—or shortly after—those meetings (and before I would make a decision to join the church), I learned that I'd been accepted to the famous institution. My father, working at the time in Aruba, was ready to fund the expensive undertaking. I would be the first in our house to go to "college."

The big problem now was finding a place to stay while attending school. And what I was about to see would be the first in a series of providential interventions in my life.

About two years or so earlier, I'd visited St. George's with my oldest brother George, and we'd stayed with friends of his on River Road, a busy thoroughfare on the other side of the hill that overlooks the St. George's harbor. So now, with the date for the opening of school bearing down upon us, we turned to this family contact, inquiring about the possibility of my staying at their place. But for reasons we never discovered, there was no response.

As the time for the opening of school approached, desperation began to set in. Which young person wants to miss out on an educational opportunity of this magnitude, simply because they did not have a place to stay? But we had no idea where to turn next. Keep in mind that we're talking about pre-Internet days, and long before people in Carriacou had seen anything close to personal telephones. Even roadside payphones did not exist. Snail mail, by boat, was the order of the day.

About 10 days before classes would begin, a gentleman by the name of Dennis Williams just happened by our home—out of the blue—to visit my mother. Williams (whom we kids knew as "Teacher Dennis," since, years before, he'd been a teacher at the Hillsborough School that we all attended) had never visited our home before, so far as I could remember. But he dropped by that day!

Knowing he'd just come up from St. Georges, my mother discussed our predicament with him, asking whether he knew of any place where I might stay. His response was immediate: "My mother takes in boarders," he said, "and she has room."

It was no happenstance; God had sent him. And He'd sent him for reasons that went beyond simply finding a place to stay. Williams' mother, Mrs. Susannah Davidson, turned out to be a staunch Seventh-day Adventist. (Does God look out for us or does God look out for us!) Had that (non-Adventist) family on River Road responded to our letter and accepted me in as a boarder, I most likely would not be giving this kind of testimony today.

It was at Sister Davidson's that I experienced, up close and personal, what it means to be a Seventh-day Adventist. While there I attended church every Sabbath, where Pastor George Riley, in his monthly visit to the church (sometimes even less frequently, since he pastored all the churches on the island) was all aglow in joy and grace as he preached. When I hear Adventists around me talk about how they were decades in the church before they learned about grace, I roll my eyes in astonishment, and thank God for the grace-filled path in which He chose to lead me. I can see Pastor Riley's smiling face still today as he exuded with the gospel on those precious Sabbaths he was at our church. And in his frequent absences, the local elders (Ogilvie, Maitland, Bonaparte, Andrews, Ince, and others—all male in those days) filled the gap with practical messages of hope and encouragement. They were each strong, joyful Christians.

Sister Davidson's first house (she moved twice while I stayed at her place) was on the Carenage, on the semi-circular street that runs along the waterfront of the St. George's Inner Harbor. You stepped outside, went across the street, and you were into the deep Inner Harbor. 20th Century Fox would select the area as one of the sites to film the popular 1957 movie, "Island in the Sun," featuring (among others) James Mason, Dorothy Dandridge, Joan Fontaine, and Harry Belafonte. Homework was hurried or left undone, as many of us students went down to the waterfront to take in the action as they filmed under huge floodlights in the evening.

From the Carenage, the Adventist church was about a half mile up the hill through a series of streets and alleyways; and when we moved to Lowther's Lane, in another part of the city, it was still close—perhaps just over a mile. Like most other Adventists in the immediate area, we walked to church every Sabbath. And as often as the pressure of school work permitted, we students also attended church on Sunday nights (for the "evangelistic service") and on Wednesday evenings (for prayer meeting). We walked in the opposite direction to the GBSS, less than a mile away. (From River Road it would have been a much longer walk; or I'd have had to take the bus, with at least one connection.)

But I almost never made it to my first class. The week I arrived, Bertram Andrews, one of the local Adventist boys, had gotten himself a small sailing boat (calling it "Salsa Negra"—"Black Sauce"), and wanted to take a few of his friends for a spin around the harbor. The venture would begin in the water right across the street from Sister Davidson's house on the Carenage; and her son Winston was one of those taking the joyride. At the last minute, as a courtesy, I was invited to tag along. It was the Sunday before school would begin.

Just as we were about to leave, Bertram discovered he'd forgotten some important item at his house, about a quarter of a mile up the hill from the harbor, and went back to fetch it. While he was gone, impatience got the better of the four of us waiting, and someone suggested we do a dry run, then circle back to pick him up.

That rash decision almost ended in tragedy. As we ventured out from the sheltered section of the harbor with sails unfurled, a wind gust pushed us further than we intended—into the open harbor—and a squall descended on us, causing the little craft to list perilously to one side. The guy at the rudder was doing his best; but that, plus the weight of the other three of us leaning heavily on the gunnels at the windward *side,* proved insufficient to prevent us taking water on the lee side. By the time the wind died down, we'd collected enough water to bring us close to sinking. And with nothing on board to bail it out, my shoes had to do. (It was fortunate that because of our hasty, unplanned departure, I'd had no time to remove them, as I ordinarily would have done.)

We did all we could to keep from sinking that Sunday morning, frantically putting those two shoes into use to bail the water. But in the end, only God's providence saved us. The same wind that had put us in such peril (and we could all have drowned that morning) now drove us across the bay to the famous Grand Anse Beach, about 8 miles, as the crow flies, from the place where we took off. As we got into shallow water, and before pulling the boat ashore, I jumped out and actually knelt down in the water to thank God for His marvelous protection. Whatever became of my shoes that doubled as a bail bucket, I do not now remember; nor can I remember how we ever got word to Bertram about the (unforgivable) mishap, how he reacted, how he got his boat back, and how we made it back to St. George's. These details are now all a blur in my mind, perhaps conveniently so (though I won't mind being filled in by the others who were present that day).

I did make it on time to the opening school assembly Monday

morning—my first day at the GBSS. And though I can't remember distinctly, I'm almost sure that the headmaster, Mr. Smith (who hailed from Barbados), probably read Psalm 133 from the King James Version that first assembly. It was his favorite text:

> "Behold, how good and how pleasant it is
> for brethren to dwell together in unity!
> It is like the precious ointment upon the head,
> that ran down upon the beard, even Aaron's beard:
> that went down to the skirts of his garments;
> As the dew of Hermon,
> and as the dew that descended upon the mountains of Zion:
> for there the Lord commanded the blessing, even life for evermore."

In many parts of the Caribbean (at least in those days), a spiritual thought, even in an otherwise secular setting, was considered normal; and for Mr. Smith Psalm 133 came in handy. It was neat, short, and seemed eminently designed to strengthen the esprit-de-corps of the boys assembled at the hilltop school. He used it often.

I was in my full school uniform—khaki pants, white shirt, and the school tie—that first day. And I made sure I wore long pants, even though shorts were also proper. In addition to the long pants, I put on the sourest, meanest face I could muster, just so to avoid the cruel initiation rites (a kind of hazing) that had become part of the GBSS culture—rites that included heavy, painful, behind-the-head raps for the entire first week, from the "old boys" of the school. The strategy worked, no one daring to mess with this mean-looking new kid.

I enjoyed my four years at the school, joining the cadet core (proving myself a marksman with the rifle in my one and only experience with live ammunition); joining the cross-country marathon for my House (and making it all the way back to the goal intact); becoming a prefect (helping to enforce order and discipline in the absence of the professors, whom we referred to as "masters"); and joining the debating team for one of the school's annual debating contests (and being voted best debater, even if my team did not win).

Latin was my favorite subject the first year of classes. Mr. Paul Scoon taught it, and I can still hear the cadence in his voice as he led the class in a vocal declension exercise of the Latin word for table: mensa, mensa, mensam; mensarum, mensis, mensis. (Mr. Scoon, incidentally, would later be knighted by the Queen of England, and would serve some 14 years as Grenada's governor general).

At the beginning of the second year of school—a time when students could switch from Latin to French, I elected to remain with Latin after attending the French class for just one period. The awkward pronunciation I heard in that first class was no match for Mr. Scoon's *mensa!* It was a pivotal decision, and one that I've regretted all my life. For whatever theoretical help with English I received from Latin, one is never wise to pass up a major living language in favor of a dead one.

All of us students at Sister Davidson's house were fortunate to have a guy named Terrence Archer (now deceased) living a few doors up the street from us. A civil servant during the day, Terrence, a veritable genius, used most of his evenings (and sometimes also Sundays) helping us with math, algebra, trigonometry, physics, French, and Latin. And he did it all for free—for the sheer joy of it. He was the kind of godsend that surfaces only once in a hundred years.

Though my father paid the bills, it was my mother who really sacrificed to keep me going. Today, one can travel to Carriacou from Grenada by plane, or by a swift-sailing hydrofoil vessel. But in my time as a student, the only way was by slow-moving schooners, powered by nausea-inducing diesel fuel. It was a harrowing, five-hour journey that typically saw many passengers lose their lunches as the vessel got roughed up by a patch of ocean we called Kick-'em-Jenny, located over an active submarine volcano about five miles north of the island of Grenada.

The ship that plied the waters between Carriacou and St. George's carried mail, produce, animals, miscellaneous other commodities, and passengers. And once a week those miscellaneous other commodities included a wooden suitcase, either *for* or *from* Roy Adams.

From, if the boat was heading to Carriacou; *for,* if it was heading to St. Georges; dirty laundry, if heading to Carriacou; clean, ironed clothes, if heading to St. George's. It represented incredible dedication on the part of my mother. With no washing machines in those days, she'd use a large tub and one of those scrubbing boards that old timers remember. Hung out in the sun to dry, clothes would quickly have to be pulled from the lines when a sudden tropical downpour threatened, and hung back out again when the system passed. Pressing was with irons on hot coals, not a pleasant task in the tropics! It was a never-ending process for her, either having to send off clean stuff or pick up dirty laundry.

She did this each and every week! What incredible devotion! What sacrifice! Just so she could take advantage of the opportunity to help her last son obtain something she never had, and which she'd have wished for all her children. For my part, I would walk the three hilly miles (round trip) each week from Lowther's Lane (the address of Sister Davidson's new place), so I could have clean clothes to wear. But it was a walk sweetened by the anticipation of the baked goodies and other treats Mom always would stash away in the container.

It was while at Sister Davidson place that I was baptized into the Seventh-day Adventist Church, one day later than the rest of the candidates. On a Sunday morning, October 5, 1958, at Grand Anse Beach, away from the eyes of the general congregation, so that word would not get back too quickly to my father who was now retired, back home, and breathing fury against those of us in the family tilting toward Seventh-day Adventism. After all, he was paying the bills for my school and board, and we didn't want to antagonize him unnecessarily.

It was a big deal to stand in front of the witnesses who'd gathered and take the baptismal vows, and be plunged into the watery grave (as we say) by the visiting conference official, Pastor Lionel Arthur. The deed was done, and I was now a Seventh-day Adventist with all the rights, privileges, and responsibilities thereto appertaining.

I moved with the Davidsons one more time—to Belmont (still

walking distance from the school); but when they moved one more time—to their own property in Mount Parnassus, about (I'm guessing) a 35-minute ride by bus (with connections) to the school, I thought it better to find closer accommodation. First it was at Sister Williams place—down the hill and right across the street from the school; and then at Brother and Sister Maitland's house, about a mile and a half away (if that far). While staying at Sister Williams', I would go with the rest of the young people of the church to our early Sunday morning beach parties, organized by Sister Winifred Granger, the Adventist Youth leader. And I remember how I would hurry back home, in time to catch the Voice of Prophecy broadcast with H.M.S. Richards, at nine o'clock. (Richards became a prominent feature in my life as a new Adventist.)

Even before I'd become a member of the church, the local members there in St. George's had drawn me into their inner circle, including me in their Sabbath School programs, worship services, and Missionary Volunteer Society (Adventist Youth) events. I enjoyed it all. But one thing bothered me. Every time I would give a talk or presentation, someone was sure to compliment me afterwards, often ending with the words: "You should become a minister."

Knowing they meant well, I would paste a smile and be polite. But inwardly I hated it. Becoming a pastor was the very last thing in the world I wanted for my life—an attitude that went all the way back to those early years when my mother—ever so gently—tried to encourage me to become an acolyte, one of those lads who, in the Anglican Church, attended the priest on Sundays during the service. I didn't want that—or anything else that had to do with priests or pastors or clerics of any kind. And now as a young Adventist, I secretly vowed that these pesky members would not be allowed to succeed where my mother had failed. So every time I'd hear the offending sentiment, I would dig my heels ever deeper into my pre-med studies at the GBSS, even if I had no idea where the money for full-blown medical studies would come from. My focus was on Biology, Chemistry, and other science subjects. I was into dissecting frogs and rabbits, making notes and diagrams of their innards, against the day when I'd have to understand the functioning of similar systems and organs in my patients.

But my studied resistance notwithstanding, the conviction kept building that perhaps these members were on to something; for their words, though unwelcome, accurately described what I also was feeling, however much I tried to smother and ignore it. *But if God really wanted me to become a minister,* I thought as I continued in a mode of passive resistance, *He'd have a big problem on His hands.* And what I was about to experience was the influence of those very hands—calm, patient, gentle, persistent.

Here's how it happened.

CHAPTER **3**

Cockroaches in My Bed—A Touch of Humor from a Patient God

THE YEAR WAS 1960; and a big youth congress had been planned by the South Caribbean Conference of Seventh-day Adventists for Port of Spain, Trinidad, with a Bible contest as one of its main features. Young people throughout the conference formed teams of two, and competed in their local churches. The local winners then competed district-wide, and those district winners would then head to Port of Spain for the rally and the finals.

I teamed up with a Lela Moore, on whom (unknown to her or anyone else) I had a secret crush in those days. It was a lot of fun preparing for the contests with her. We won both locally and district-wide, and so were off to the finals. My first time on a plane, I found the 45-minute flight to Port of Spain that Friday afternoon next to my attractive teammate one of the coolest things to ever happen to me. But it was much too short.

That evening Caribbean Union youth director Pastor Milton Neblette spoke, the meeting held at the Stanmore Avenue Church, the largest Adventist church in Port of Spain at the time. He brought a powerful sermon on the second coming of Christ (parts of which I still remember), and the special music by a youth choir when he was done burned its way into my soul. The song is more than a hundred years old as I write, but its message moves me still:

"Jesus is coming to earth again; what if it were today?
Coming in power and love to reign; what if it were today?
Coming to claim His chosen bride, all the redeemed and purified,
Over this whole earth scattered wide; what if it were today?
Glory, glory! Joy to my heart 'twill bring.
Glory, glory! When we shall crown Him king.
Glory, glory! Haste to prepare the way;
Glory, glory! Jesus will come some day."

Adventist parents (and Adventist churches) might be encouraged to know that when they fork up hard-earned cash to send their youth to spiritual events like the one I was attending—that those young people often return with positive memories that last a lifetime. I can't tell you how often I've re-lived the emotion of that Friday evening and felt again the spiritual impact of that closing number from the youth choir. I think it probably had something to do with what we call "the moment." A young lad in a brand new country and city, sitting all showered up among fellow youth on a Friday evening, with all the expectations of a beautiful Sabbath and weekend ahead of him. That sermon and that youth choir struck home with me.

That night in the private home they'd arranged for me, I slept, as they say, like a log.

Pastor Glen Maxson, then youth director for the Inter-American Division of Seventh-day Adventists (headquartered in Miami), delivered the sermon Sabbath morning at Queen's Hall, near the Savannah in Port of Spain, with hundreds of youth and others present. At the end of his message, he invited those to stand who felt the call of God to serve in a variety of capacities and professions—as nurses, teachers, missionaries, etc. I sat there nervous, anticipating the discomfort when he would arrive precisely where I knew he was headed: *ministers*. I was determined to keep my seat and sweat it out. And that I did.

The Bible contest happened in the afternoon. Lela and I came in second. In other words, we did not win. An outcome that (for me) had a very pleasant result, for it made my teammate break down in tears on my shoulder in the garden at the back of the auditorium—something that never would have happened if we'd won. You get my drift.

What weighed heavily on my mind as I got into bed that night, however, was not the result of the contest, but rather the appeal following the morning sermon, and my response to it. I'd felt keenly convicted as Pastor Maxson was making the call, but had stubbornly refused to respond. Now it all was coming back to me.

Just try and sleep it off, I told myself, *and you'll feel better in the morning.*

But I couldn't fall asleep. About five minutes after turning off the lights, I sensed the presence of critters crawling all over me. In a mad rush, I flung out of bed and quickly turned the lights back on, only to see cockroaches chasing in all directions. A single cockroach unnerves me. But nearly a dozen of them! Helter skelter, I killed as many as I could with my slippers, then remained sitting on the bed for a while, pondering my predicament.

Finally, I shake the sheets, turn over the pillows, search every corner, turn off the lights, then gingerly roll back into bed a second time. But just as I begin to doze off, an encore performance! Loads of crawling vermin again! Lights on again, and slippers put into action again, as I begin to worry about waking up the entire house.

That was the same room and the same bed in which I'd slept undisturbed, like a log, the night before. So what's going on tonight? That was the thought going through my head when, suddenly, in a flash, I got it. I was trying to sleep off a conviction that had been building for years, and God was trying to tell me something. Those cockroaches—both in number and behavior—weren't normal. God had sent them.

I got down on my knees and said: "God, if you want me to go into the ministry that bad, then the answer is yes. And thanks for the cockroaches." Then turning off the light one more time, I rolled into bed and slept like a log, as I did the night before. *No more cockroaches!*

The skeptic in me would have taken this story with many grains of salt, were someone else telling it. But it happened to me! I left Port of Spain more convinced than ever about the reality of God and His intervention in our personal lives.

It was a radical decision I'd made in that Port of Spain bedroom. Literally overnight, my entire future changed. And the big question now was where to go from there. Already my head was spinning as my teammate and I flew back to St. George's, with nary a word from me about the drastic transformation I'd experienced in the night. I must now find a way to attend the church's college that trains pastors for that region, Caribbean Union College (CUC) (now the University of the Southern Caribbean) in Trinidad. And I must switch course from pre-med to theology.

It was in those post-congress days that I sat for my Higher School Certificate (HSC) exams, administered by Cambridge University through the GBSS. It was also in those days that I made application to attend CUC, with all kinds of protracted arrangements for the transfer of academic credits and so forth.

Having been accepted at the college, I headed for a teaching stint in Tobago, Trinidad's sister island—to raise funds for school. While working in Tobago I would receive word from Lela, by prearrangement, that I'd passed the HSC, the highest exam offered at the GBSS. With no telephone in the house where I was staying, I'd sent her the number for a payphone up the street from us, and that's where (overjoyed!) I took her call that morning. It was now early 1961.

Teaching high school in Glamorgan, Tobago, was an intriguing experience. Fellow teacher (Barbadian) Clyde Richards and I would spend some six months in the place, staying at the home of the principal, Mr. Charles Williams, next door to the school. The two of us slept in a single room that was so narrow you could almost touch both walls with arms outstretched. When we opened up our cots at night, there was hardly any space to walk between them.

It was an outdoor toilet situation; and we took our daily bath in a nearby river—about 10 walking minutes away. On the few occasions we ventured down to the beach about half a mile away through coconut fields, we were like two fraidy cats, not daring much beyond knee-deep, ever mindful of the much-publicized drowning death of a ministerial intern on the island not long before we came. The fact that it was a black-sand beach made it all the more foreboding. You couldn't see what lurked beneath the surface.

Meals came with our living arrangement at the principal's house; and although some kind of drink came with the daily fare, we stayed away from the local water itself, which, for some reason, we distrusted. In place of water (get this), we sucked on oranges for the entire six months we stayed there! (Incredible! And, in retrospect, very unhealthy.) Old Brother Beesman (if I get the spelling of his name right) had given us unlimited access to his nearby orange grove, and we took advantage of the privilege.

We both taught a variety of subjects. Mine included Spanish, of all things, since there was no one else available to teach it. I'd taken the subject at the GBSS, and now the onus fell on me. Even so, I kept hoping and praying I wouldn't have to deal with the preterite tense before the school year ended. And I didn't. For some reason, the preterite in Spanish has always given me trouble. (Incidentally, the fact that I once taught Spanish has been a topic of mirth in our house, especially with a wife who hails from Panama. I can remember a time when she and I would talk to each other in Spanish, so our kids wouldn't understand. But with the language receding from my mind for lack of use, I lived to see the day—after our kids had themselves taken Spanish in school—when she and they would communicate in Spanish so *Dad* wouldn't understand. Go figure.)

In Tobago I preached my first sermon. It was in the lead-up to local elections, and the Glamorgan Church had permitted just one political party to hold their planning meetings on its premises—in our elementary school in the church's basement. I remember that that open association with party politics on the part of the local church came in for strong, unfavorable mention during that maiden homily.

The experience in Tobago behind us, both Clyde and I headed for CUC to begin our ministerial careers.

CHAPTER 4

On to CUC... and into God's Widening Providence

THERE'S A GOOD taste in my mouth whenever I think about the two years I spent at Caribbean Union College (CUC—now University of the Southern Caribbean), with a great bunch of fellow students and with stellar teachers like Linda Austin, Lucy May Kum, G. Ralph Thompson (later to become secretary of the General Conference), and George W. Brown (later, president of the Inter-American Division). I still remember the huge psychological lift I would receive in Elder Brown's classes when a term paper would come back with the letter "A" on the title page, sometimes embellished with the expression, "Excellent!" or "Splendid!" What an enormous boost to a struggling student's morale!

To tell all the details about my time "in the Valley" (as alumni frequently call their alma mater, nestled in the midst of the Maracas hills) would require space not available here. But as I write, several events and experiences come to mind.

Friday evening vespers, for example. That was truly the highlight of the week. One felt relaxed, following six days of study and work; sitting there in those comfortable seats in the old auditorium; joining in the lively song service; receiving a spiritual message; and being lifted to another level by special music from a talented groups of singers on campus at the time—students like Jules Agasson; Meade James; Shirley Christiani (now Shirley Baptiste); and a spectacular male quartette (Durant George, Sylvan Noel, Otto Tol, and Jacques Le Bonne)—"a perfect mix," Vernon Andrews called them in an email to me, "one Tobagonian, one Grenadian, one Surinamese, and one Martiniquan—representing English, French and Dutch."

One favorite of the quartette (a song written by Ina Duley Ogdon about a hundred years ago) filled me with the deepest inspiration every time I heard it:

"When you my Jesus understand,
When you accept His loving hand,
A happy morn will dawn for you
When you know Jesus too.

When you know Him, when you know Him
You'll love Him just as others do;
A happy morn will dawn for you
When you know Jesus too."

Only when you match those words with the music can you get the full impact of what I'm saying here. It makes one fall in love with Jesus all over again. That was vespers.

And after all that, there was yet something else to look forward to on a Friday evening: sack-lunch. At midday, each student picked up their stuff for supper: a loaf of fresh whole wheat bread baked that very day; a chunk of cheese; a small packet of sugar; some margarine; a small can of evaporated milk; a hefty slab of natural, creamy peanut butter (bringing peanut punch to mind for many students); and one hard-boiled egg. In those days, scrumptious stuff! How I'd like to turn back the clock and enjoy one more Friday evening at CUC just as it used to be in the old days, with the identical batch of students and faculty—just one more Friday evening!

One of the most memorable events for me while attending CUC took place off campus. A group of us (Pathfinders, Pathfinder leaders, and a few members of the faculty) made the exhausting hike over the Maracas hills and down to Maracas Beach on the other side for a camp-out. After setting up camp for the night a short distance from the beach, the first thing we did was fix lunch (each team had lugged the materials and supplies they would need). I remember that in my team someone (who shall remain nameless, so as not to embarrass myself) put too much salt into the huge pot of dumpling and peas, spoiling the entire batch, and turning our group into sudden welfare recipients.

Immediately after lunch, we headed down to the beach on full stomachs (which was the first wrong thing we did).

Our second mistake was to fail to do what the Pathfinder's handbook said we should, namely, that before swimming in unfamiliar waters, you test the current. Instead of doing that, dozens of us, anxious to get the show on the road, plunged in immediately.

Within five minutes, no less than 13 Pathfinders were drowning simultaneously. The water close to shore was fairly shallow, but the breakers were high, and the under current very strong. So when the waves came, they knocked you over; the current pulled you under and out to sea; the grade rapidly dropped, and suddenly you found yourself in deep water and in big trouble.

Pathfinders were screaming everywhere for help. Those of us who were taller or were better swimmers struggled to help the others. Meanwhile, both the Pathfinder director and the president of the college (I can see them still as if it were yesterday) are standing on the shore chatting away, without the foggiest idea anything was wrong. They thought the kids were just having a ball.

I remember hearing my roommate say as he came up for breath: "Roy, help me!" But by that point I'd already helped several others and was feeling so absolutely exhausted I didn't think I could make it back to shore myself—which was *just there!*—less than 12 yards (11 meters) away!

I know now how a person feels just before they die, because I expected to die that afternoon. A multitude of thoughts go through your mind in seconds—in my case thoughts of my mother; of my other relatives; of my girlfriend back on campus—her reaction when the news got back that Roy had drowned. All those and a hundred more raced through my mind in seconds. Then, suddenly, a huge wave came and pushed me into shallow water.

I shouted to the others: "My roommate's out there! My roommate's out there!" And quickly we formed a human chain, our strongest swimmers at the deep end, and pulled him in; then spent the next 20 minutes trying to drain the water from his lungs.

No one drowned that day, thank God! But that experience marked the end of the beach party for us. That evening at worship, you should have heard the singing. I think if we were camping over a graveyard, we'd have raised the dead. We sang as young people who knew they'd just been plucked from the jaws of death. Back on campus, we had a story to tell.

The president on that Pathfinder trip was B.G.O. French, one of the two college presidents in my time on campus. He'd followed B. L. Archbold, a story teller par excellence. Once, when trying to encourage us boys to keep our clothes clean, Archbold told about the boy who would never wash his trousers. So one day, when he took it off, "the trousers stood up," Archbold said, stiff with dirt. French, for his part, put much personal energy into his chapel talks—-as when, focusing on Psalm 84:5-7 in the King James Version, he went through some five chapel periods, squeezing out every last nugget from the passage ("Blessed is the man whose strength is in thee; in whose heart are the ways of them. Who passing through the valley of Baca make it a well; the rain also filleth the pools. They go from strength to strength, every one of them in Zion appeareth before God"). It was fascinating to watch him draw lesson after spiritual lesson from the text.

There's so much that happened during those two years at CUC that I cannot tell in detail. About the time, for example, when, following a Sabbath morning appointment in south Trinidad, a group of us made an after-lunch visit to the world-famous Pitch Lake, where I lost a good pair of church shoes, coming away thankful that I didn't myself sink down into the place. It happened when, curious about a little shack standing nearby, I'd momentarily veered away from the group to check it out. In doing so, I inadvertently left the hard surface of the lake and, without warning, found myself venturing onto the soft, sticky portion. My shoes got stuck, and I was glad to abandon it for firmer ground, riding back to campus in my socks alone.

Or about those Saturday evening socials down the Maracas Road, hiking with your favorite person; or about the night when Montezuma's revenge hit the campus, and how I was spared because, not liking the looks of the soup the evening before, I didn't take any; or about the play I wrote and directed, that completely flopped; or about canvassing in St. Lucia (during the summer of 1962), and staying (together with Clyde Richards again) at the home of the Calendars, their house surrounded with huge, luscious, ripe avocados!

Also, with the passage of time, some details have gone from memory. About that canvassing stint in St. Lucia, for example, I wish I could remember what happened when I appeared at the home of Mr. J. Q. Charles, one of the wealthiest men on the island in those days, only to be confronted at the end of the 50-yard driveway by two huge dogs, each close to half my height. How did I handle those dogs? Did the residents let me in? Did they buy my book(s)? Did I ever meet Mr. Charles in person? Those details have gone from me. And how did I fare when I arrived in the town of Vieux Fort, on the island's southern end, to stay at the dilapidated house of an elderly Adventist brother living alone and with no food in the house, except a loaf of bread with mold beginning to grow on it? Who was this elderly man? And how did I come to stay at his place? Why wasn't Clyde with me? How long did I remain there? Did I sell any books? How did I survive in the town? All those memories have fled.

What I do remember, however, is that it turned out to be a good summer, and both Clyde and I went back to CUC for our final year with scholarships.

The first chapel assembly that second year made a most powerful impression on me—because of one item on the program that day: the special music by college registrar Mr. Clayton Enriquez. And though I've referred to this detail elsewhere in my writings, I think it bears repeating here to round out the present picture. I would doubt that a single other student present that day remembers the selection. But I do. Perhaps because of the particular issues in my life at the time, the message of his song burned its way into my soul, and I feel its power still today. With humility and much grace, he sang those powerful words and music created by C.S. Briggs long ago (and how I wish every reader were familiar with the tune, so the full impact could come through):

My life goes on, some days are good, some ill;
O Father, let Thy loving presence fill
Both day and night; O hold me so I cannot fall,
For thou art Life and Strength, And All in All.
Hold Thou my hand, dear Lord, Hold Thou my hand;
I do not ask to see, or understand.
Only that Thou wilt be constantly near to me,
Holding my hand, dear Lord, holding my hand.

Only in eternity will Mr. Enriquez learn what that song has meant to this lone student over the years.

The moments that linger warmest in memory are the worship services. The occasion, for example, when music professor and college choir director, Vernon Andrews, led the choir (of which, for whatever reason, I was then a member) in singing that immortal favorite:

The king of love my Shepherd is,
Whose goodness faileth never;
I nothing lack if I am His,
And He is mine forever.

The piece comes in a variety of tunes and arrangements. But the one used that day (which, I understand, was a favorite of B.G.O. French) was that by Harry Rowe Shelley. For me, it's the most moving of all the tunes, evoking a multitude of powerful images as, with all parts blending, we came down to (what I call) the tranquil moment of the piece:

> Where streams of living water flow,
> My ransom'd soul He leadeth,
> And where the verdant pastures grow,
> With food celestial feedeth.

Finally, the piece crescendoes for a dramatic ending:

> And so, through all the length of days,
> Thy goodness faileth never;
> Good Shepherd, may I sing Thy praise
> Within Thy house forever!

It gives me goose bumps still today as, nostalgically, I hear the music in my head as we presented it that morning.

Yes, the worship events made a huge impact. But the social times did not fall far behind. I remember those Saturday night marches on what we called "the slab," a concrete pavement (an oversized tennis court) outside the boys' dorm. As the function would come to an end, one could see boys' dean Mr. Kenneth Ford standing at the parting of the ways, to ensure that the boys stayed on their side of the campus, with the girls proceeding to their quarters *unescorted.* That always brings a chuckle in retrospect.

I remember being president of the men's club (The College Spartans) at the same time that my girlfriend was president of the women's club (Alpha Delta Chi). I remember the big banquet we staged during our concurrent presidencies. That night, as a keepsake, each of the seven couples at the presidential head table (not all of whom were "dating") signed their names on each other's programs. I kept mine, and years later would notice that just one of those seven couples eventually made it to the altar—and it was not the presidential couple.

As pastor of the 1963 graduating class, I remember our class's early Sabbath morning worships—something like 5:30 a.m., followed by our pre-sunrise hikes down the cool Maracas Valley Road. What precious social memories! Of course, the fact that my steady was also a member of the class heightened the joy of it all. That year, 1963, would turn out to be a big year for her. She would both graduate from college and become engaged. We announced our engagement at an alumni-sponsored banquet at the Port of Spain Hilton the Sunday night after graduation.

A few days later, college church pastor and professor Elder G Ralph Thompson, who'd played the informal role of advisor to us during the past year, drove us to Piarco Airport as she left for home. Franck Pourcel's "I Will Follow Him" (later made famous by Whoopi Goldberg in "Sister Act") was playing over the airport's PA system as we hugged goodbye and she made her way through the departure gate. The song had come out earlier that very year (1963), and as Little Peggy March with her back-up troupe sang it that day, it was as if the words had been composed for that very moment, and especially for us. My fiancée would follow me wherever the path led, and I her. It was, in a sense, our song, cementing our love and devotion forever. She would "always be my true love," and I hers.

But were we just dreaming? Only time would give the answer.

Caribbean Union College! The school quickly grew on me. I didn't miss the GBSS a single day while I was there. And the place left a mighty good taste in my mouth.

CHAPTER 5

Port of Spain, Tobago, and a Frightening Journey to Canada

I WAS ONE of the fortunate ministerial students to receive an internship appointment before graduation. It was to Port of Spain, to work with H. E. Nembhard, senior pastor of the Stanmore Avenue and Woodbrook Adventist churches. Stanmore, as indicated earlier, was the venue of that Friday evening vesper service that had so impressed me years earlier during the weekend of that conference-wide youth congress; and Woodbrook was a good-sized congregation, sharing the same grounds with the South Caribbean Conference.

So mine was what some might call a plum assignment. But the place of my first assignment really didn't matter much to me. For undergirding my thinking as I went out was an image I'd seen more than a year earlier on the cover of *The Youth's Instructor* of January 2, 1962—the picture of a young man holding an uplifted Bible and standing in the hands of God, with the cover caption reading: "In thine hand... to make great." Taken from 1 Chronicles 29:12 in the King James Version, those words (strengthened by that cover image) served as a beacon urging me forward, regardless of my placement or the immediate circumstances around me.

It was during this time in Port of Spain that I first met Peter Prime (who'd just graduated with a degree in theology from West

Indies College—now Northern Caribbean University—in Jamaica). Both of us were beginning our formal ministry and internship with Pastor Nembhard. [Prime would later serve as president of the South Caribbean Conference; then president of the Caribbean Union; and still later as associate secretary of the General Conference (GC) Ministerial Department. As it turned out, we would both begin and end our ministerial careers together, retiring almost in the same year from the GC.]

My first time in the pulpit at Stanmore Avenue was at a Sunday evening service, with Pastor Nembhard sitting on the rostrum behind me. I had rehearsed the sermon all Sunday afternoon, speaking to the dead folk at the Woodbrook Cemetery, close to the apartment of Sister Maude Lewis, where I stayed. I remember the service that evening; but what has completely (and perhaps conveniently) faded from memory is what happened after an awkward gesture on my part sent my sermon notes flying in all directions.

Things were all uphill after that inauspicious beginning, and I had many other occasions to redeem that initial fiasco. But my stay in Port of Spain would not be long. I was soon re-assigned to Tobago, there to intern with a veteran Adventist minister, Pastor Maurice A Joseph, whose wife, among other things, made sour-sop drink that was to die for.

It was from this Tobago location that I would begin to take some nerve-racking risks—nerve-racking only in retrospect, however; for at the time I was doing only what I thought I had to do. And it was during this period that I would experience—again and again—God's kind and timely providences. I sometimes tremble when I look back.

Peter was with me at the conference office as I called British West Indian Airways (BWIA) to book my flight to Tobago for September 30, 1963—on their first run, departing at 8:30 a.m., as I recall. (Those were the days when I could move from one pastoral post to another with all my belongings in two suitcases.) "Why don't you take the afternoon flight," he said to me while I was still on the line with the airline, "instead of leaving so early in the morning?" It made sense, and I immediately suggested they put me on the afternoon flight instead. Turned out that had I left on the morning flight, I'd have arrived in Tobago just in time for Hurricane Flora, a wicked storm that passed directly over the island with winds at more than 100 miles an hour, causing considerable destruction, and damaging the home where I would have been staying. What that change of flight saved me from I will never know this side of heaven, but I'm eternally grateful to Peter, who long since would have forgotten the incident, except that I keep reminding him of it from time to time.

I eventually made it to Tobago in November, my second stint on the island (the first time, you'd recall, as a high school teacher). This time, I located in Canaan on the island's south-western tip, staying at the home of Sister Merita Roberts. From my monthly check of $95.00 (in those days the conference subtracted the tithe before sending out workers' paychecks), I had to pay for rent and board, take care of regular necessities, and try putting a tiny bit away for the proverbial rainy day.

Pastor Joseph (affectionately known to many of us as JoJo) was a joy to work with. He was almost perpetually late for appointments; but however angry you felt for being "stood up," sometimes for an hour or more, his broad, calming smile and apology when he eventually turned up melted you away.

My first church experience with him was at a Wednesday night prayer meeting at which I spoke. A business meeting followed, with him in the chair, to discuss, among other things, readmitting into membership a man who'd been disfellowshiped after a moral fall. When the man's own brother objected to the move, arguing that the candidate had not shown sufficient evidence of repentance, JoJo put a question to him that I've never forgotten over the years: "Are you the recording angel?"

Catching the brother off-guard, the question silenced him, and the meeting voted the re-admittance. The encounter told me something of the depth, fearlessness, and compassion of this senior pastor with whom I'd come to work. One Sabbath, as I preached at our

Mt. Pleasant church, not far from where I lived, I wanted strongly to express my disgust at something or other (cannot for the life of me remember now what that was). But instead of saying: "I don't give a dime for ...," I found myself actually saying: "I don't give a damn..." Startled to hear the strange expression coming from the preacher's own mouth in front of the saints on the Sabbath day, I gratuitously came at the same point a second time, just so I could say it right this time, with the hope that people might think they'd misheard me the first time.

Still not sure I'd fixed the damage, I found JoJo later that very Sabbath—ahead (I hoped) of any ear-witnesses to the verbal flap—and told him what my own tongue had done to me that morning. Leaning back in the seat of his car, he laughed: "That means," he said, "that you were on fire with the message!" I chuckled with him, and felt assured that with JoJo my reputation was in good hands. That's the kind of man he was.

I learned to drive, stick shift, in Tobago; and I remember the day a fellow intern let me take a short spin alone in his vehicle on the main road that goes through Canaan. And I remember how I panicked when it dawned on me that I'd not yet learned how to shift into reverse—and so, how would I turn the car around? Anxiety sweat had just begun to flow when I recalled that at the airport, not far away, was a traffic circle. I did the extra mile to the place, made the circle, and so was able to return the vehicle, without my colleague ever discovering my predicament.

Just after receiving my driver's license and purchasing my first (used) car, I headed out one Sabbath morning for an appointment in Charlotteville, clear on the northeastern end of the island. Sister Roberts, perhaps out of personal safety concerns, declined my invitation to ride along; and so, alone, I headed out for the place, driving up and up into the hills, before I would descend to my destination near the sea on the other side. I was to reflect on the wisdom of Sister Roberts' decision when, cresting the hill and approaching the first curve, I dozed off momentarily. Awaking with a start, I found my hands already turning the steering wheel to the left, away from the steep, precipitous, and clearly fatal drop that was awaiting me.

God's angel had done it again! His mighty hand was in my life.

It was while in Tobago that the letters from my fiancée stopped coming, a development that, to say the least, left me utterly confused and devastated. Meanwhile, the yen for further academic studies kept growing inside me—faster now, since any prospect of an immediate wedding (which had been our plan) was looking more and more like a distant dream.

But how does a ministerial intern making $105.00 a month in the local currency (there had been a big raise from $95.00) come up with enough funds to enroll at Andrews University, which in those days was requiring a deposit of U.S. $1000.00 (about 6,135.00 TT$, as I estimate it for that period)? It seemed an insurmountable problem—until word came to me (through some channel I cannot now remember) that the publishing department of the Canadian Union of Seventh-day Adventists had developed a program through which foreign students could earn canvassing scholarships in Canada during the summer, with the money earned going directly to the Adventist educational institution of the student's choice.

Wasting no time, I immediately made application to the Canadian Union, receiving a surprisingly prompt response. I was accepted into the program, but was presented with an unexpected condition: I needed to deposit with the union sufficient funds for a return trip to the Caribbean, should my efforts at a scholarship fail. So not only did I now have to find enough money for the trip to British Columbia, my assigned province, but also enough funds to bring me back home, if that became necessary. I'd graduated from Caribbean Union College with a small credit from my canvassing scholarship the previous summer; but adding that to my meager pastoral savings allowed only for a plane ticket to Miami. It was not enough for me to fly to Vancouver, let alone provide for a return ticket to Trinidad.

With the summer months bearing down on me (it was now about the middle of May), I wrote to my sister Flossie for help. It seemed to take forever, but one Friday afternoon a money order from her arrived from the UK—too late, however, for me to reach the bank to make the transfer before closing time that day. But the banks were open Saturdays in those days; so what should I do? The summer was upon me (it was now late May), and time was of the essence. Should I consider a Sabbath visit to the bank an "ox in the ditch" situation?

After mulling it over, I decided against it.

But I was literally the first in line as the bank opened Monday morning. "I want to send a money order to Canada," I said to the teller.

"Sorry, Sir," came the devastating response, "Canada is outside the sterling area [I'd never heard the expression in that context before], and we're not allowed to send funds from here."

Crisis. Bewildering and unexpected. What was I to do now? It seemed that all my hopes and plans were crumbling at my feet in one single instant. I stood there at the window stunned, dazed, confused. Mercifully, at just that moment, the phone rang, distracting the teller, and giving me a moment to pray. "The Lord hear thee in the day of trouble," I silently breathed the promise, "the name of the God of Jacob defend thee; send thee help from the sanctuary, and strengthen thee out of Zion...(Ps 20:1, 2, KJV). (I know there's no magic in the text, but it's a powerful promise that I've claimed at critical moments in my life, and God in the past had come through for me.)

"Why do you want to send this money to Canada?" asked the teller when she reappeared after the phone call.

I opened my mouth and two words came out: "Student deposit."

"Oh," she said with obvious relief for my sake, "we can do that."

Wow! Ain't God good! Where did those two unscripted words come from? I left the bank that day with a renewed understanding of the reality of God's mysterious presence in my life. I felt as if guided by invisible beams of light, sent directly from the throne of God.

I don't remember now the exact date, but sometime after receiving word from Canada, but before that nervous day at the bank, I'd informed South Caribbean Conference officials of my plans to take a study leave. As I was to discover, any talk about study leave in those days was something akin to heresy. Perhaps it was deemed irresponsible, given the shortness of time and the number of workers needed for the task. Why would I waste time and money on higher education when there were souls to win and a world to warn?

I couldn't be sure what exactly motivated these officials at the time, but I was clearly getting absolutely no encouragement over my plans for further study. I do not remember receiving a single word of support or blessing or well-wishes from anyone at headquarters. When I went to the treasurer's office a day or two past the middle of June (1964), I naively expected to be paid for the full month, having budgeted those extra dollars into my plans. Instead, it seemed as if the treasurer calculated my pay down to the very minute I left my assignment in Tobago; not a penny more. Nor was there a single iota of concern for what should have appeared to him as a foolhardy journey on my part into the unknown. Since that day, the thought has often crossed my mind: *Was there no scholarship fund from which he might have spared a few dollars for this ambitious joker? Or even a petty fund put aside for Christmas knick-knacks and other trivia that might have contributed even a hundred dollars to help this struggling soul?* And to think that that particular treasurer had come to his present office from the education department, in which function his visit to my home church in St. George's had been one of the factors that encouraged me in the direction of CUC, which, in turn, had whetted my appetite for further studies!

That day I left his office deflated and discouraged. But it was too late to turn back.

I had no difficulty disembarking from Trinidad. For all the immigration officials there knew, I was traveling locally, within the Caribbean region, on to St. Lucia first.

I was making a stop in St. Lucia to get a handle, once and for all, on the status of my relationship with this girl to whom I'd been engaged. That's where the conference had assigned her as a Bible worker. I found the place where she stayed—at the home of the local

Adventist pastor in the place. It didn't take me long to figure out that it was all over, and so our meeting was very brief. Within a half hour I was gone from her house, satisfied as I left that our relationship was dead and, moreover, should never be revived. For us, the words of that song at the airport, "I Will Follow Him"—had been a mirage.

So it was with a heavy heart that I flew out of St. Lucia en route to Antigua, the burden of this new development adding to what I was already feeling from that experience in the conference treasurer's office in Trinidad. Antigua would be the stop where I was to board an American Airlines flight for the trip to Miami. Without sufficient funds to purchase a ticket from Trinidad to Vancouver, my plan was to fly to Miami, then travel across the U.S. by bus to my destination. It was a perilous undertaking that, in retrospect, makes me tremble.

The entire plane was held up in Antigua, as American Airlines officials debated what to do with me. Turned out I didn't have the proper in-transit documents to land in the United States and travel through its territory to Vancouver. If I were refused entry, American Airlines would have to foot the bill to get me back to Antigua, a prospect they obviously did not relish.

It was a crisis exponentially more unnerving than the one I faced at that bank in Tobago. For there in Tobago, had I been unable to send the money, I would simply have signaled the South Caribbean Conference that there had been a change of plans, and then continued my work (though perhaps under a cloud of suspicion). But here in Antigua, if I were turned back, I hadn't a clue what on earth I would do. I'd abandoned my work with the conference and, at any rate, did not even have enough money in my pocket to get back to Trinidad. If you've never been through a moment like that, then you have no idea what stomach-wrenching fear grips you. There couldn't have been anyone else on earth that day feeling more helpless. It was as if all my hopes and dreams were about to collapse at the American Airlines' boarding gate.

But in that moment of extreme crisis, God came through—*again!* All I know is that after about a 45-minute delay, God moved on the heart of some unknown official to give the OK for me to board. I now approached the entrance of the plane, fully expecting all eyes to be on the culprit that was responsible for the long delay. Humiliating stuff! As I plopped down into my seat, I breathed a long, long sigh of relief, grateful beyond words.

Even so, there wasn't much time to savor the providential development, for the next anticipated crisis was only four hours away. And as the plane approached Miami, new fears arose. Will I be allowed to enter the country? Will the concerns of those airline officials in Antigua materialize? Will I be sent back? And if so, back to where?

We land. I follow the line of passengers. Anxiously, I await my turn. I approach the immigration counter. Within seconds, the official stamps my passport. I'm in! Not a single question asked!

Do I believe there's a God? Where's the person who can convince me otherwise?

If this manuscript ever sees the light of day, then let me say that the lines you're reading right at this point did not come easy. As you read, it would be impossible for you to see the long pauses I'm experiencing at my computer, struggling to find appropriate language to describe my feelings as I look back upon that critical day. I'm completely wordless at the moment, and the frightening "what ifs" still give me the chills.

But it turned out right; and all I can say is: *Isn't God awesome!* Again and again I've felt the presence of His heavenly light, the guiding power of His invisible hand.

It was Friday when I arrived in Miami. And I'd made arrangements to spend the Sabbath at the home of (let's just say) a minister whom I'd known in Trinidad. It was the old days of segregation—in the south, especially—and the minister was living in a Whites-only neighborhood. As a consequence, I was politely advised to keep my head down, as it were. No strolling in the neighborhood, for instance; no sitting out on the porch. Indoors was the name of the game. On Sabbath morning, I discretely entered and exited their vehicle from a side door under the carport.

The restrictions, notwithstanding, I was glad for a place to stay, and will eternally be grateful to this minister and his family for that extraordinary act of kindness. They arranged for the Inter-American Division under treasurer to take me down to the division office Saturday night to do a money exchange. He gave me U.S. currency for all the Trinidad money I had; took me to the Greyhound Bus depot to purchase a ticket for Vancouver; noted my arrival time in Vancouver, and promised to send the information to the local conference there. The value of such assistance was priceless—absolutely priceless.

Early the following morning, I set out by Greyhound for the 5-day journey to Vancouver with the money I had remaining after the ticket purchase—*just over $8.00 U.S!* Yes, you read that right—just over e-i-g-h-t dollars in United States currency! The tiniest leniency on the part of that conference treasurer in Port of Spain would have made a huge difference now. The Greyhound bus always seemed to stop where the food was most expensive; and I really had to scrimp.

I would learn many things during that trip, one of them being the strong racial divide in the U.S. at the time, affecting washrooms, restaurants, and other facilities along the way. I remember the day when, unconsciously behaving as if still in the Caribbean, I was innocently following the (white) crowd into a restaurant near the bus depot. Stopping me cold, the most pointed index finger I'd ever seen directed me back outside and toward a wicket in the wall, through which Blacks were served. I also had to stand outside to eat, or find a seat on some outside bench somewhere or on the grass. And I marveled at the patience of African Americans who've had to put up with such humiliation and indignity all their lives. In the midst of all this, however, a friendly white woman one day, out of the blue, surprised me by buying lunch for a Black (uniformed) military serviceman and me. (Only later would I understand the significance of this unexpected kindness.)

There could be few things more boring than having to sit on a Greyhound Bus for five days, night and day, day and night. It's worse than watching paint dry. Finally, with the Canadian border approaching, my heart starts pounding once again; and sure enough, my premonitions materialize. As permission to enter Canada, I'm carrying a letter from the Canadian Union, authorized by the Canadian government. But the immigration officer at the border does not recognize it and, accordingly, would not allow me into the country.

Every new crisis seemed tougher than the one before it—first at the bank in Tobago; then at the American Airlines departure gate in Antigua; and now this! The nightmare of being turned back now was beyond comprehension. The entire Greyhound Bus is held up just because of me, as I try to reason and plead with the official. "Why not call Ottawa," I at last suggest, "and verify the authenticity of the letter."

Surprisingly, he agrees.

But if you ever have tried to reach a human being in a government office—and a human being able… and willing to help—then you will understand the extraordinary statement that follows now: *The officer on the British Columbia border phones Ottawa; gets a human being; AND that bureaucrat in the Canadian capital happened to recognize the authenticity of the letter I was carrying, giving the clearance for me to proceed!*

How astonishing is that! If you were me, would you have the words to describe it? I don't.

Leaving the immigration office that afternoon, I headed toward the Greyhound Bus with my things, with all eyes looking (as in Antigua) to see the culprit who'd been holding things up. But however humiliated I felt, I entered that bus bubbling over with gratitude for God's amazing providence.

"The LORD HEAR THEE IN THE DAY OF TROUBLE; THE NAME OF THE GOD OF JACOB DEFEND THEE; SEND THEE HELP FROM THE SANCTUARY, AND STRENGTHEN THEE OUT OF ZION" (Ps 20:1, 2, KJV).

British Columbia Conference publishing secretary, Elder Walter Bergey, was waiting for me at the bus station in Vancouver, and took me to his home in Mission City (35-40 miles away) for the week-end. As I'd spent money for meals day after day on the road in the United

States, I purposely had avoided looking to see how much remained of the $8.00 with which I'd left Miami. I didn't want to get discouraged. But that Friday evening after worship and supper at the Bergey's, I went back to the little room they had for me, and for the first time dared to look to see how much remained. There was nothing where the bills should be, so I looked in the little change pocket to find what was there: $0.33. Yes, thirty-three cents! Only then did I understand why the Lord had moved upon that kind Caucasian lady to buy me lunch that day.

The next day was 13th Sabbath, and I put all 33 U.S. cents into the Canadian offering plate, understanding from experience for the first time what Jesus meant when He said of the widow that "she, out of her poverty, [had] put in everything—all she had to live on" (Mark 12:44). *So here I was in a strange country without a single red penny in my pocket! Nothing!* It was a defining moment. For it wasn't simply that I didn't have one red penny *in my pocket;* it was also that I had no money whatsoever, anywhere!

Penniless in a new country. In retrospect, it scares the daylights out of me. Who else but God could pull off a thing like that! What but His mighty hand could provide such precision guidance? On the one hand, it makes me tremble—still. On the other hand, it makes me feel like shouting "Hallelujah!"

"I will sing to the Lord, for he has been good to me" (Psa. 13:6).

CHAPTER 6

Heading to CUC Number 2...and Sensing God's Continuing Providence

THE NEXT DAY, Sunday, as he drove hundreds of miles to get me to my first assignment, Pastor Bergey, after giving me all kinds of canvassing tips, regaled me with tall tales about the coldness of the Canadian winter. In the winter, he said, the voices of lumberjacks freeze as they work out in the bitter cold; then in the spring, as things begin to thaw, their voices unfreeze, and could be heard echoing all across the forest.

Other such humorous tales, combined with the picturesque beauty of the British Columbia countryside, helped make the 280-mile journey less tiresome.

He took me to the City of Williams Lake, setting me up in the home of Dr. Art and Mrs. Keitha Spenst. Monday morning, on foot and without a single penny in my pocket, I knocked on the first door, just down the street from the Spenst's house. The residents were home (on a Monday morning!); they invited this stranger in; and they bought a set of *Uncle Arthur's Bedtime Stories* cash. Now my wallet was no longer empty. There were 34 Canadian dollars in it!

Just think about that for a minute: the very first home visited in the country; invited in; cash sale! It was as if the Lord was saying to me: "Roy, I'm with you! Hang in there."

It would be impossible adequately to recount the many kindness-es shown me by Canadian Adventists—and Canadians in general—during that first summer in the country. When the Spensts needed to leave town for a while, they made arrangements for me to stay next door, at the home of Pastor Allan and Mrs. Dorothy Robertson. Pastor Robertson was the pastor of the Williams Lake Adventist Church, and when he and Dorothy also had to leave for camp meeting (in the beautiful town of Hope), they entrusted their home and pantry into the hands of this perfect stranger.

What generosity! And what trust!

At camp meeting there were special arrangements made for col-porteurs, including student colporteurs; and for the two weekends of the meetings that year, I traveled to the place, driving both times with Brother Harry Bechtold, one of the local elders of the Williams Lake church, a very spiritual, warm, and engaging person. As we would drive those 246 miles (396 kilometers) to the camp meeting site, I would sometimes hold my breath as Bechtold, at break-neck speed, negotiated the frightening curves of the mountainous road, eating sunflower seeds all the way, splitting them open with his teeth— "to keep alert," he said.

After arriving on the campground that first Friday afternoon, I visited the Canadian Union College trailer, and liked what I heard. The required deposit for new students was $250.00 (compared to Andrews University's $1000.00), an attractive offer for this church-rat poor student. I signed up on the spot.

And so, in one fell swoop, my plans to attend Andrews University changed. Now it was on to Lacombe, Alberta, to attend Canadian Union College (now Canadian University College)—CUC number 2.

Before that, however, there'd be much canvassing work to do. Joined later in the summer by a student from the Bahamas, I was moved from Williams Lake to Kelowna, where Pastor Bergey intro-duced us to the Knellers. We would stay at a little place they provid-ed—a converted garage, they called it; a stand-alone, ground level apartment, equipped, as I recall, with a stove, a refrigerator, and a few other amenities.

"Where's the toilet?" my canvassing colleague wanted to know.

"Oh, let me show you," the publishing secretary said, taking us outside and pointing to a little shack about 20 yards (18 meters) away.

It can get cold in British Columbia during the night and early mornings, even in the summer; and when Bergey showed us the outdoor facility, my friend's countenance visibly fell. Humorously trying to console him, Bergey said: "If I had a dollar for each time I've had to use an outdoor toilet, I could be a rich man today."

My Bahamian friend was gone inside of 10 days (an episode he and I have since had occasion to laugh about). But I stuck with it, eventually developing a friendship with an elderly Adventist sister living not far from the "garage," at whose home I would go many evenings for a few minutes after my canvassing day, to eat strawberries and raspberries, topped with evaporated milk and honey. Scrumptious!

The summer ended; I'd done well; and now it was on to Canadian Union College.

I remember the dread I experienced as, from the train heading into the city of Red Deer (some 15 miles from the college), I saw snow falling for the first time. Clad only in the jacket I'd brought from the Caribbean, I almost panicked. Education department chair, Dr. G. A. Graham, picked me up in the wee hours of the morning and took me to the college, where a very unpleasant thing immediately happened—perhaps the only one during my two-year stay on campus.

Instead of getting me settled into my room as quickly as possible, the assistant dean of men (he might have been a *student* assistant), in those ungodly hours, took this tired, anxious soul into the dean's office to admonish him as to how he was never to date the white girls on campus! (From that point in 1964, it would be years—if not decades—before the first black female would show up on that campus. And so his admonition began for me a two-year dating hiatus which, as the months went by, became a badge of achievement of sorts—a record I didn't want to break.)

Perhaps that assistant dean was reacting to something that had happened not long before in Toronto, 2000 miles to the east, with connections to that very campus. The date was 1960, four years earlier; and (Barbadian) Alfred Greaves, a recent Canadian Union College theology graduate, had arrived in Toronto and announced plans for his upcoming wedding. Greaves was Black; his fiancée (whom he, apparently, had met at CUC) was white; and therein lay the root of the crisis that would develop.

The wedding was to be conducted by the (Caucasian) pastor of the Pauline Avenue Seventh-day Adventist church in Toronto, where many West Indians went to church; but at the last minute, with the wedding party and guests waiting in the sanctuary, the pastor failed to show.

So far as I know, the full reason for this incredible snub is still shrouded in mystery, but the prevailing assumption was that it had something to do with race, and that the pastor was responding to orders from on high (and I'm not talking about heaven). In the midst of that terrible humiliation, someone called a local Baptist minister, who saved the day for the severely embarrassed couple. The incident made headlines all across Canada, and perhaps that overly zealous assistant dean was doing his best to forestall any new incidents of the kind.

As schools go, Caribbean Union College was my first love. Nothing could supersede it. But now came Canadian Union College, my second CUC. It was a great experience, but different. That first winter turned out to be the coldest since 1892, they said, with the wind-chill temperature for a couple of days falling to an incredible -49° Fahrenheit (-45° Celsius). A few of us senior students lived in a campus apartment, with the men's dormitory between us and the school's cafeteria; and I remember that on our way to the cafeteria (just about 50 yards—46 meters--away) during that cold spell, we were forced to make a stop in the Men's dormitory to warm up, before finishing the short remaining distance to the cafeteria.

It was a tough introduction to the Canadian winter.

I'd entered Canada on what would have been a temporary guest worker visa. So now that my plans had changed, it would mean applying for a student visa while already within the country, something that was usually taboo. Canadian Union College officials assured me, however, that it could be done and that they'd stand with me until the issue was resolved. But it made for considerable nervousness whenever I saw a Royal Canadian Mounted Police (RCMP) vehicle arrive on campus. *Might they be coming for me?*

They never were; and in time the situation was resolved. One of only four black students at the time (all male), I nevertheless felt fully integrated into the life of the campus—except that I found it prudent to keep that assistant dean's early-morning warning about dating ever at the front of my mind.

One day, not long after settling in as a student, a letter arrived from British Columbia—from a Mrs. May Turner. I'd met her and her daughter, Donna, in the cafeteria line at Hope camp meeting during the summer, and we'd sat together for the meal. It was a most cordial visit, in which, naturally, I talked about my (new) plans for attending Canadian Union College.

Now a letter had arrived from this dear lady, whom I'd never expected ever to see again or hear from. She wanted to wish me well in my studies, and to send a little something to help in my expenses. Enclosed was a check for $1,000.00!—a huge sum in those days, and a giant boost to my morale, especially as I'd begun to wonder whether the scholarship I'd earned had enough lifting power to tide me through that first school year. Eventually, I would call her Mom, and we'd become life-time friends. I attended her funeral on Vancouver Island in December of 2009.

The following Summer I was back in British Columbia, experiencing a reunion, of sorts, as I linked up with Clyde Richards again, with whom (as mentioned earlier) I'd worked in Tobago high-school teaching and in St. Lucia canvassing. Our first assignment was in the city of Prince George, near the eastern center of the province. Here we had a standing Sabbath lunch invitation to the home of the Schneiders, near the banks of the Fraser River, where their Chi Wawa brought us endless entertainment, grumbling like a bulldog ten times its size, every time he saw anything that might vaguely be construed as a hostile move on the part of the two strangers.

After leaving the Prince George area, we arrived late at night in the town of Vanderhoof (about 60 miles to the west), and headed to the home of the elderly sister, where arrangements had been made for us to stay. But she'd already gone to bed, and not all our knocking—on doors and windows around the house—could rouse her. Eventually assuming no one was home, we bedded down as best we could in our car for the night. (If you ever wanted to understand how vital stretching is to a good night's rest, just try sleeping crouched up in a car all night.) Our sister woke early the next morning to find a strange car in her driveway. She'd heard nothing of our ruckus during the night.

From Vanderhoof we traveled 296 miles (477 km) north-west to Terrace for the final stop of the summer, staying at the home of an Adventist dentist in the town, whose kindergarten-aged daughters would see black faces for the first time. Misjudging the distance as we headed for the place in my 1948 Pontiac, we got there much later than expected—close to midnight, actually. Just before entering the town, we came upon a single-car accident that, apparently, had just occurred. The vehicle had gone off the road in a wooded area. As we stopped to give assistance, we were surprised at the first words out of the mouth of the (apparently drunk) Native Indian man standing beside it. "I know you guys are church guys," he said, uncannily assessing these two perfect strangers in the midnight darkness of the place. "Please don't report this to the police." It gave us a sense of having an invisible divine mark on us as we headed into our final assignment for the summer.

It was another tough but successful summer, ending with a young Adventist couple not only purchasing my vehicle, but also giving me a ride in it at no cost—all the way back to the college in Lacombe, 900 miles away, where they were to pick up a vintage antique vehicle to take back. For a poor student looking to save every dime, this was an unexpected providential development; and I've often reflected on the monumental kindness of this couple, whose name I no longer remember. It must have been a sacrifice for them, traveling with two restless primary-aged girls. After the first 15 of the 900-mile journey, one of the girls piped up from the back seat: "Daddy, are we almost there?" It was the first in a series of queries those poor parents had to endure throughout the long journey, once the two rascals were awake.

I was returning for my second and final year at the college (1965-66), one that would be chockfull of activity. And thinking ahead, I began making contact with various church entities in regard to the possibility of sponsorship to Andrews University. Starting (in December) with my home base, the South Caribbean Conference, I explained in a letter to President Arthur L. Ward that I was set to graduate the following May, and was inquiring about possible sponsorship to Andrews to study toward (what was then) the Bachelor of Divinity degree (today, the MDiv). I explained that Andrews had just changed the BD program from three years to two, making summer work for enrollees very difficult, if not impossible. Did the conference have any provision for sponsorship? (I'd shouldered the first degree all on my own, and didn't consider the request unreasonable.)

Alas, I didn't hear back. Not a squeak.

J. W. Bothe, then president of the Canadian Union, did respond to my letter of inquiry, written months later (when I'd given up on ever receiving a response from South Caribbean). Unfortunately, however, it was to inform me that he could not "hold out any hope" for me at that time, since "all the vacancies were spoken for by the various conferences." Inter-American Division president, C. L. Powers, suggested that I contact my local home union in Trinidad, but noted that "it is not customary for us to grant a bursary ... to a worker who has not spent considerable time laboring in the field." Better to return to the Caribbean Union "with the understanding that at some later date definite arrangements will be made to grant you educational assistance in harmony with the bursary plan." Elder E. E. Cleveland went to bat for me with the Regional Conferences in the U.S., but in the end was unable to secure anything.

Meanwhile, campus life had to go on. I would join the college's temperance contest, win it, then head to Atlantic Union College in Massachusetts for the North-America-wide finals, coming in second or third (as I recall); I would serve as editor of the campus newspaper (*The Aurora*); and would be elected president of the graduating class, a role that placed me at the center of all the class activities that year.

I will never forget the extreme loneliness that descended on me following graduation, when the seemingly ceaseless round of activity suddenly came to an end. Perhaps no group of students anywhere in the world vacates a campus more rapidly than Canadian Union College students. From an activity level of, say, 95, it went for me all the way down to about 5 in one fell swoop, leaving me utterly drained, deflated, and alone.

But it wasn't to last long. Within 48 hours, I would hitch a ride with fellow-student Bill Hafner in his tiny car (have long since forgotten its make and model) for the 2000-mile trip to the Adventist headquarters in Oshawa, Ontario, carrying all our earthly belongings in that small space on wheels. We drove by day and slept in parks or some other open space at night (whether in sleeping bags or crouched up in the vehicle by the roadside—when we couldn't find an open space—I cannot now remember). We freshened up at gas station washroom facilities in the mornings. Arriving in Oshawa after four rough days on the road, we were glad to bed down in the dormitory at Kingsway College, its students having already left for the summer.

While canvassing in Ontario, I broke off on the weekends to attend the General Conference session in Detroit's Cobo Hall, where my former professor (and at that time Caribbean Union president), G. Ralph Thompson, put me up in his room—a generosity on his part that only later I came to fully understand.

In Ontario, I'd headed into my third summer of canvassing in Canada, this time with Andrews University on my mind. There I would work on my Bachelor of Divinity degree. In my final months at Canadian Union College, I'd applied to (what was then) the Ontario-Quebec Conference for sponsorship to Andrews, but there had been no response. So that as I canvassed in Ontario and later enrolled at Andrews, I understood I'd be doing it all on my own. It would be an expensive undertaking, even though I was still single.

But all that changed when I was called out of class one day to meet with Pastor Phillip Moores, president of Ontario-Quebec, who gave me the good news that the conference had decided to sponsor me.

It was a development that would change the rest of my life, bringing me assurance of future employment in the ministry. Ever since I'd vacated my job at the South Caribbean Conference, the prospect had been uncertain. For not only was there no expression of good will on the part of conference officials upon my departure, but my letters to them had all gone unanswered. It had concerned me that not a single communication from my home field inquired after my welfare, or expressed any hope of my return to help in the work—which was fully my intention when I left. Now another conference had stepped in to fill the gap, and I was most grateful. God had come through yet again!

CHAPTER 7

Finding That Special Girl ... and Pastoring in Canada

EVER SINCE THE day I faced the reality of a broken engagement in St. Lucia while on my way to Canada, a frequent sentiment of my prayer was: "Lord, where's that special person for me? Where does she live? And how do I find her?"

The prospect of finding her was put on hold during that two-year dating hiatus at Canadian Union College. Getting to Andrews University, I dated several young women, but without ever experiencing a this-is-the-one moment. I remember the girl (a music major) who, after insisting we attend a chamber music concert in Seminary Hall one Saturday night (rather than the more attractive regular lyceum in the university auditorium), proceeded to fall fast asleep during the event. I was not impressed.

On another occasion, with a different date, I found the young lady spitting mad when I arrived an hour late to take her to a Saturday evening function. It was my fault entirely. After preaching that morning in South Bend, Indiana (at a church to which a colleague and I had been assigned as student pastors), I'd stayed back for lunch and for the youth meeting, forgetting that Michigan (the location of the campus) was running one hour ahead of Indiana that time of year. It's often a critical detail when it comes to appointments, but one very easy to forget. In this case, I'd totally forgotten. And, my apologies and explanations notwithstanding, our relationship went south from there.

There were others that at one point or the other had looked somewhat promising. But in the end, I finished my degree without landing that special person.

Now it was on to Toronto—and the year, 1968.

While searching for an apartment after arriving in the city, I stayed temporarily at the YMCA on College Street in downtown Toronto. I have no idea how I came to attend a hootenanny at the Toronto Junior Academy auditorium north of the city one Saturday night during those days; but while at the program, I spotted a young woman who simply blew me away.

I was with an old friend from Andrews, and the young woman in question just happened to be hanging out with my friend's sister. "Who's that young lady with your sister?" I asked him. "Do you know her? Can you introduce us?"

I recalled spotting her in the choir loft months earlier during a visit I made to Oshawa (from Andrews), when she was appearing as a junior at a capping ceremony for senior nursing students. I'd made a mental note, but had had no opportunity for a meeting. Now, here she was again, in the company of my friend's sister.

Casually, as if nothing was afoot, we meandered to the place where they were. First, he introduced me to his sister, then to the young woman in question. Taking all of half a second, she responded: "Hi" (no exclamation mark in her voice), then immediately turned away to follow the activities up front. I'd ceased to exist, for all she cared. And my thought was: *Wow! How do I fix that?*

Learning that she was a student at the Branson Hospital School of Nursing (next door to the hootenanny venue that night), I contacted the women's dean, introduced myself, and asked if she might not want someone to take one of their evening worships. (The strategy was that as I greeted the "congregation" after the meeting, this young lady was sure to come by, giving me the opportunity to say—however cornily, "Hi! Didn't I meet you at the hootenanny a couple Saturday nights ago?" Then I would play it by ear from there.)

The dean was delighted at the idea—who in her position wouldn't welcome such an offer from a young area pastor, providing her a little break for a change? The evening worship, as I recall, was to be at 6:30 p.m.

Looking at the map of Toronto I had with me, I noticed that the School of Nursing was almost a straight shot up Bathurst Street; and in my ignorance, I estimated the time it should take to get from the Y to the place—only about 13 miles away. On the appointed day, well-rehearsed, I set out for the school, totally unaware of the gridlock of Toronto's rush-hour traffic. As I traveled up Bathurst, I sometimes found myself waiting through as many as three light changes to cross a single intersection. By the time I made it to Branson, worship time had long since passed, and I found myself apologizing profusely to the dean for the no-show.

Graciously, she understood, extending the invitation to a future date, and giving me another opportunity to recoup from the disaster. For the new appointment, you can be sure I left the Y with plenty of time to spare. But what became of my scheme is a total blur in my mind. All I remember is that I did get a chance to meet the young lady somehow, and that by the time I was transferred to Montreal not long thereafter, I had established enough contact to send her a cryptic message in the mail, one carefully calibrated to stir up her curiosity in such a way as to compel a response. (How I wish I could find a copy of that document now—to refresh on how I actually worded it!)

It worked. And several months later I managed to persuade Sister Linda Parchment, the senior pastor's wife (whose daughters were friends with the young woman in question), to extend an invitation for her to visit Montreal. I was in Ninth Heaven when she showed up, and proud as a peacock when we entered church together that week-end. I can even remember the brownish floral dress she was wearing, matching her complexion completely.

The story is long. But the short of it is that eventually I got the girl, as we say: Celia Mercedes Wilson from Panama! We were married in early September some two years later, with a honeymoon planned for Barbados, contingent upon her receiving a renewed Panamanian passport. Traveling all the way to the embassy in Montreal only to discover that the document had not arrived, we were forced to opt for a Canadian venue instead. That's when I talked her into a destination that, from seeing pictures of its rustic surroundings, had always fascinated me: Halifax, Nova Scotia.

There I would expose my young bride to the first big embarrassment of her married life. Arriving late at night at our hotel, we approached the desk together. "What's the name, Sir?" the clerk politely asked. And as the self-appointed spokesman for the duo, I answered without missing a beat: "Roy Adams and Celia Wilson," momentarily forgetting that her name had just been changed.

My wife was mortified.

"O, sorry, Sir," I said, catching myself and hurrying to fix the damage, "I mean, Roy and Celia Adams." And the clerk was like: *O yeah, Tell me another story!* (Where are those sinkholes when you need them?) As we left the counter, Celia demanded we move to a different hotel the following day. And we did, going on to spend several enjoyable days in the exotic city.

Celia was now (as they say) "a pastor's wife," the last thing she thought she'd ever be. Though not an up-front person, she nevertheless got along just swell with the members of the East Toronto Adventist Church, where I was senior pastor. They loved and respected her. One reason was that when I encountered rough times—at board meetings, for example—I would shield her from the barbs hurled against me, telling her only those details that would keep her in the know on the essentials. It was a strategy that often would confuse and puzzle members who, after lambasting her husband during a board meeting, ran into a genuinely friendly pastor's wife on Sabbath morning. They couldn't figure it out! I've always held the view that pastors can unnecessarily prejudice—if not damage—their spouses (and eventually themselves) by sharing too many negative details of events and meetings. It can often lead to needless anger and resentment on the part of the spouse, who can, in sympathy, easily exaggerate a situation much beyond what was intended.

Every pastor encounters strong emotions and opposition on boards and committees—it goes with the territory. But my mention of barb-hurling in that last paragraph was only to make the larger point about keeping the ministerial spouse above the fray. But the truth of the matter is that during my days as a pastor I encountered nothing but respect from the members of the churches where I pastored, operating from the principle that if I treated everyone with courtesy, they'd tend to reciprocate. It worked. And part of respecting leaders on boards and committees was keeping their occasional temper tantrums to myself and not infecting my wife with them. Once they caught on to that single strategy, it exponentially increased their respect for me.

Incidentally, I adopted the same attitude vis-à-vis the matter of members' problems told to me in confidence. I remember once visiting a couple who were going through a bitter family matter, ending in the husband leaving home. When the wife called my home to give me a follow-up report, I was away. So she proceeded to speak to my wife instead, beginning (as it were) in the middle of the story, with the assumption that I'd already briefed her on their situation. Reacting to my wife's puzzlement, the sister said: "Didn't Pastor Adams tell you?" I suspect that her respect for both of us heightened when she learned that I'd held their confidence intact.

By the time I arrived at the East Toronto Church, I'd interned with four senior pastors—H. E. Nembhard in Port of Spain (for about four months), Maurice Joseph in Tobago (for about eight months), Rudolf James (upon my arrival in Toronto—about three months), and Earl J. Parchment (in both Montreal and Toronto—for a total of just over a year and a half).

It was sheer joy to work with these four men, each one a Christian gentleman. It seems a tragedy to me that (as it happens all too frequently) a ministerial intern would be thrust into their assignment with no mentoring; which makes me feel so blessed that I had not just one, but four totally different models to learn from. There are all kinds of stories I could tell about my time with each of them, stories arising from our mutual experiences and from the vignettes they shared with me from the wealth of their individual journeys.

One story that comes to mind happened upon my arrival in Montreal to join Pastor Parchment. Shortly after getting there, I went to the bank to open an account.

"Occupation?" the bank official asked as she filled out the appropriate form.

"Pastor," I said.

"What church?"

"Seventh-day Adventist," I replied.

But the name was so totally unfamiliar to her she just could not hear it—even after I'd said it three times. Finally, I had to write it down for her.

The incident left me with the strong conviction that something must be done to publicize our presence and the name of our church in Quebec's largest city. And later that day I shared with Elder Parchment an idea that came to me as I drove away from the bank that morning. With the winter approaching, I said to him, we could organize our Pathfinders for service, outfit them with special winter gear, with the name "Seventh-day Adventist" emblazoned on the back of their jackets. We would get radio and television stations to announce their service as the snow descends, shutting in thousands of infirm and elderly people who could not dig themselves out. It would lead to public-service announcements from media all across the huge metro area: "Call the Seventh-day Adventists." And as these young heroes went to work, television cameras would pick up the logo on the back of their jackets: "Seventh-day Adventist Pathfinders."

Remarkably, when I shared the plan with Pastor Parchment, he took it with a straight face, even if he'd already spent several winters in Montreal. For my part, I was familiar with winters in many places, but was yet to experience one in that French city. I was living at the time in an apartment on the service road of the Decarie Blvd, a major 8-lane corridor through one part of the city. To get to my apartment if I were heading home on the Boulevard from downtown Montreal, I would have to pass my building (to my left), travel about a quarter of a mile, take the exit ramp, cross the bridge over the highway, then turn left and drive back to the apartment building, now on the right of the service road.

The first snowfall was unexpected and caught me on the boulevard heading home from downtown. As I crept by in heavy traffic, I could see my apartment building to the left. But it would take me about 90 minutes just to do the quarter mile, clear the exit ramp, cross over the bridge, and make the left turn back to my building. When I finally made it home, cold and frustrated, I called Elder Parchment. "Elder," I said to him, "remember that plan for the Pathfinders I shared with you about three or four weeks ago?" He did. "Well," I said, "I don't think it'll work." And I shared the experience I'd just had.

Parchment laughed out loud in the hearty way he does. He'd known it all along, but had said not a discouraging word. He waited until I discovered the total impracticality of the plan for myself. That's leadership—wise leadership; understanding leadership. And even at that point, he wasn't laughing at me, but with me. Still today, I get a chuckle when my mind goes back to the hare-brained idea I'd drummed up way back then.

My first evangelistic meeting in Canada was in Montreal, in a rented hall, with the full support of the senior pastor and the congregation—though I cannot now remember the results in terms of baptism. I do remember, though, the cooperation of the young people of the church in all aspects of the meetings.

In retrospect, I think I probably came across as an activist to some people, while I worked as a pastor in Canada. For me, however, it was just a spontaneous participation in what I considered important community affairs. When I learned, for example, of a forum in downtown Toronto on the subject of the spirit world, sponsored by *The Toronto Star* (one of the two large newspapers in the city at the time) and featuring (among others) the well-known journalist-author-psychical researcher, Allen Spraggett, I immediately made plans to attend. I went simply to learn. But when a University of Toronto professor, opposing Spraggett's affirmation of unexplained psychic phenomena, conceded that if he were to see a ghost tomorrow, he'd change his tune, I knew I had to speak, given all we understand as Adventists about spiritualism and the state of the dead. My comments appeared in the *Toronto Star* the next morning, with me being identified as the pastor of the East Toronto Seventh-day Adventist Church. Not a bad way, however inadvertent, to get the name of the Adventist Church in the news.

Years later, when the Ontario business community began pushing the Ontario Provincial Government to enact legislation making Sunday what they called "a common pause day"—thus avoiding (in their thinking) the religious connotation, the Provincial Government arranged for hearings in various localities to receive community input on the issue. Infiltrating what was perhaps the most prestigious hearing of all, in downtown Toronto, I managed to get permission to read a (hastily prepared) paper on religious freedom in opposition to the move by the united business group. In contrast to the thunderous applause following the speeches by business representatives, only a whimper followed my remarks, coming from the small pocket of Adventists from my church who were able to show up during working hours on a Monday to support me—and perhaps from the single Jew in the audience (who'd also presented a paper in opposition).

My wife and I went home that afternoon disappointed and dispirited. But the following day, to our surprise—all the thunderous applause for the other presentations apparently going for naught, it was my speech that was quoted extensively in news stories of the event in the *Toronto Star* and in the city's other large newspaper, the *Globe and Mail*, with *the Globe* also treating the issue in its lead editorial, associating my name with the Seventh-day Adventist Church.

But Toronto was (and still is) a very secular town, one in which native Torontonians don't so much oppose you as ignore you. And that prevailing attitude has had an impact on Adventists in the city. Based on purely anecdotal evidence, I've often said (thinking particularly of the city's Caribbean immigrant population) that if one could gather all the Adventists in the metro area, who are no longer attending church, one could easily organize at least five new congregations of 300 members each. In preparation for my first evangelistic effort in the east of the city as a young pastor, we handed out thousands of flyers. And I still get a chuckle at my naiveté on being surprised to encounter a thousand headlights heading in the opposite direction, as I headed down the Don Valley Parkway that first night. *Why aren't they all coming to the meeting!* It was probably crazy of me to have expected those handbills and those meetings to make even the slightest dent in that secular metropolis.

But I was determined to learn the evangelism ropes as best I could, however difficult the situation in that secular city. And although, with others, I welcomed the coming of big-name preachers like E. E. Cleveland and George Vandeman to the city, I wanted such efforts to alternate with my own in the local area of my church. That attitude brought high tension one day in a meeting of Ontario Conference officials with all the Toronto pastors. It was a meeting called to organize a city-wide effort, with veteran evangelist Henry Feyerabend leading out. Having already developed my own evangelistic plans for that particular year, however, I expressed my desire to stick to them, little anticipating the amount of pressure I would encounter to flow with the tide. Surprisingly, conference president Phillip Moores, sitting in the chair, came to my defense. "If Roy wants to have his own meetings," he said, "I think we should support him."

I was like *"Whew! What was all that opposition about?"*

Yet if the president had not intervened, I would have had yet one more card to play, and that would have been to take the matter back to my church board and to a business meeting—where I would have been in the chair.

I think that when I arrived in Canada, I was only the third black Adventist pastor in the entire country—all three of us of Caribbean heritage. And there were just two churches with majority black members, one in Montreal (the historic Westmount Adventist Church, boasting prominent Adventist pioneers among its founders); and the other in Toronto—the Toronto West Adventist Church, which celebrated its 50th anniversary in 2013. Founded by Caribbean immigrants, it became "the mother church" for West Indian émigrés, giving birth to a multitude of daughters over the years. It's the church where I did my longest pastoral internship, and the place where Celia and I got married in 1970.

The East Toronto Church once was almost (if not) completely white some time before I got there. And although we intentionally strove to win new Caucasian converts during my time, only a few ever came. But the old-time Caucasians still remaining in the congregation were among the nicest people, though generally on the elderly side.

For a while, the small Portuguese church in downtown Toronto also fell under my care; and the typical Sabbath found me rushing home to Willowdale (in the north) for lunch, then hurrying back downtown in the afternoon at breakneck speed, to take the Portuguese service. The language barrier made for some interesting dynamics at nominating committee time, in particular. As chair, I would simply sit there dumb, listening to the discussion in Portuguese; then ask, when I sensed it was over, "So what's your pleasure?" And the first elder would clue me in on the decision. I enjoyed my time with them.

We'd grown to love the city and it was hard to leave when the time came. We left a part of our hearts there; and it still feels like going home whenever we have opportunity to visit.

CHAPTER **8**

Going Back to Andrews— a Scary Journey

The material in this chapter first appeared as "God's Timing" in God Answers Prayer, a small paperback published by the Adventist Review back in 1997. It's a vital part of my story and needed to appear here. I've made additions here and there, and several minor changes to the original text.

"THE LORD HEAR thee in the day of trouble; the name of the God of Jacob defend thee; Send thee help from the sanctuary, and strengthen thee out of Zion" (Ps. 20:1, 2, KJV).

As I've said before, there is no magic in these words. They are not some good luck charm or fetish. But when, in times of trouble and extreme danger, I have appealed to God on the basis of the promise contained in them, God again and again has come through for me.

I had been a pastor in the Ontario Conference for several years, and was beginning to feel a little rusty. When I made the decision to return to Andrews University for postgraduate studies, I knew the risks of announcing my intentions to the church before I was absolutely sure. For once having done so, as every pastor knows (and however much the saints love you), you thereby pass the point of no return.

But despite our efforts to operate in compliance with that reality, things did not fall into the correct sequence and events did not develop as expected. Thus it was the Monday following the announcement to the congregation of our departure that my wife and I appeared at the office of the U.S. Consulate in downtown Toronto, seeking the appropriate entry visas. We carried with us the items they'd requested—bank documents and other papers—as proof of our net worth. We anticipated a positive outcome.

However, in less than five minutes after we appeared at the counter window of the immigration supervisor, she'd reached a negative determination. "Mr. Adams," she said curtly, "we don't think you have sufficient means to support a wife in the United States. You can go, but she can't." And that was that. She was done with us.

Stunned and with heads down, we walked away, knowing that going back on our announcement to the church was not an option. We had to leave.

December 31, 1974, would be our departure date. And several men from the church came over the night before to help us pack and load our things. My wife and I would drive our own vehicle—loaded to the hilt; and my brother-in-law, Simon Lazarus, would follow behind us in a U-Haul truck.

As we left Toronto in the predawn hours of that winter morning, heading west on Highway 401, one overwhelming question haunted us: *How do we cross the border together, with all our household goods—I with an I-20 (student) visa and Celia with nothing to show? Where is the immigration officer who wouldn't suspect hanky-panky and send us packing* (no pun intended)?

Before leaving, we had discussed various entry options. We'd toyed, for example, with the idea that one vehicle could enter via the Detroit-Windsor Tunnel (which links Windsor, Ontario to Detroit, Michigan), while the other would enter about two miles west, by way of the Ambassador Bridge. Once inside the United States, we could reconnect for the rest of the journey. Eventually, however, we decided against any subterfuge. We would sink or swim together.

About 100 miles out of Toronto, I looked in my rear view mirror and felt a sudden tightness in the pit of my stomach. The U-Haul was covered in smoke. That was about 7:00 a.m. It took about an hour and a half to get a tow truck to pull the fully loaded beast to an auto repair shop in Woodstock, the nearest town.

As we waited, with nothing to do but twiddle our thumbs, the clock kept running. Nine o'clock. Ten o'clock. Eleven. Twelve. The mechanics broke for lunch. But one of them—out of concern for our predicament—returned half an hour early to continue the task. About 45 minutes later, however, he came to us with terrible news: "The engine is shot. It's not going anywhere."

If you've ever found yourself utterly numb with discouragement and frustration, then you can understand our emotion upon receiving this dreadful intelligence. Perhaps providentially, I was down with laryngitis and virtually incapable of doing any verbal damage to anyone.

Forced into renting another vehicle (can you sense our plight? Can you picture our misery?), we chose a larger truck this time. Even so, it took backbreaking work to make the transfer, one or two of the mechanics helping us. Finally done, we hit the road again. It was now about 4:00 p.m.

As we finally drove through the tunnel under the Detroit River into the United States, our hearts were pounding. *What will happen to us now? We've given up our apartment and cut all ties with both church and conference in Ontario. What if we are turned away? How can we go back?* It was an exceedingly nervous time, a moment of deep apprehension.

The U.S. agent guarding the border gate took one look at our papers and directed us inside the immigration building—almost never a happy development. Within minutes, the officer inside had made a determination dead on target with that of the agent in Toronto weeks earlier: *Entry denied for spouse.*

I have no problem being attended to by women at banks, supermarkets, and all kinds of other businesses and establishments. But when crossing borders—-or dealing with any other kind of immigration or customs issues—I try to stay clear of them. For some reason, not a few of the ones I've encountered in those particular settings have been unbending, unreasonable, legalistic, even insulting. It was a woman (a supervisor, to boot) who'd attended to us in Toronto; and as bad luck would have it, it was another woman now facing us down in Detroit.

Entry denied for spouse!

It was a dark moment. A million thoughts raced through our minds, the fundamental one being: *What do we do now?*

We requested to see a supervisor.

"You may see the supervisor," she said bluntly, "but he'll tell you the same thing."

"May we see one, anyway?" I insisted.

As we waited, I sent up a silent petition on the basis of the promise of Psalm 20:1, 2. *"At this critical hour, O God of Jacob, send us help from the heavenly sanctuary."*

At that very time, an incident was developing near where we stood. A young Canadian hippie was trying for the third time that day to enter the United States to attend a rock concert in Detroit, armed with such documents as library identification papers and service-station-issued fuel charge cards. Refused entry once again, his frustration took a quantum leap; and in an angry voice he referred to the border officials as "a bunch of pigs."

In making that comparison, his choice of animals, admittedly, was not the best. But he really had not broken any law—no more than if he had called them a bunch of eagles or sparrows. But that porcine comparison so offended the official standing at ground zero of the young man's rage, that he grabbed him by the back of the neck and pushed him out of the building, across the open space, and through the turnstiles to wait for the pedestrian tunnel shuttle back to Canada.

And the official in the thick of this heated disturbance was none other than the supervisor, the very one we were waiting to see. Returning to his desk, and knowing full well that he had badly mishandled the situation, he felt the psychological need for understanding and atonement. And we were next in line.

As he opened our papers to examine them, his mind was clearly still on the unpleasant incident just concluded. Unloading some of his frustration, he looked to us for sympathy. Whatever his interpretation of our completely inarticulate grunts, he was ready within 60 seconds with his determination, signing our documents "OK," and sending us back to his subordinate, who was to stamp our papers and complete the process.

Taking one look at what he'd done, she barged into his office to confront him. "How could you do this," she scolded. "According to section [so and so], subsection [so and so], those people should not be allowed into the United States." She was hopping mad, and we could hear her voice from the other room as we waited at the counter.

But she'd chosen the wrong time to scold a powerful guy who'd just made atonement (of sorts) for a grievous sin. Banging his hand on the desk so loud we could also hear it from where we stood, he exploded: *"I said they can go!"*

Crestfallen, she came back to us and, however reluctantly, stamped our documents. We were on our way!

Well, almost. There was just one little hurdle left: customs.

As I thought of all the packing and loading in Toronto, and the unloading and reloading in Woodstock, I dreaded the prospect of doing it one more time there at the border. But we had no choice. Handing over the key to the agent, we watched as he proceeded to open the truck's container door.

The moment he pried the fasteners loose, some glass trinket we had placed at the very entrance, in our hurry, fell to the pavement and broke. It was not the agent's fault, but he did not know that. Utterly embarrassed, he simply shut the door and waved us on.

We were in!

I still get goose bumps as I look back now upon those tense moments. Who but the God of Jacob could have arranged such perfect timing? After all kinds of mishaps and unexpected delays, who but the mighty God of the sanctuary could have landed us in that supervisor's office at that precise moment? God's miraculous providence had come through once again.

My wife, while living in the U.S., was able to secure the necessary papers to regularize her status. We stayed five years in Michigan, and I finished the doctoral program with a credit balance, even though our family, during the same period, had grown by two. That supervisor in Toronto thought it couldn't be done, but God had the last word.

CHAPTER 9

Caught Up in a Theological Crisis: My Experience with the Doctrine of the Sanctuary

AS MENTIONED EARLIER, I wasn't born into a Seventh-day Adventist family. I joined the church as a teenager, experiencing huge opposition from my father who, after working decades abroad, had now returned home to Grenada.

I was baptized while attending school in St. George's; and for most of the year, I was practically away from home and out of my father's supervision and control. So when I would return home for brief holidays (Christmas, Easter), I reasoned that the best approach would be to not upset him unnecessarily, given the brevity of the period; and since I could do what I wanted the rest of the time while away. So rather than going to church while at home, I would go out into the fields and keep Sabbath by myself. I would take my Bible, the Church Hymnal, and the Sabbath School Quarterly with me, find a shaded spot under some large tree, and stay there for hours.

My favorite section of Scripture during those times was the book of Hebrews. For whatever reason, I found myself completely fascinated with the epistle as a young Adventist, often just simply mulling over its pages, reading it and reflecting, with my thoughts on heaven.

Later, as I began to pursue a ministerial career, I started hearing all kinds of rumblings and innuendoes about the doctrine of the sanctuary, which, of course, is a central theme in the book of Hebrews and also a cardinal teaching of the Seventh-day Adventist Church. There were whisperings, insinuations, and snide remarks—as if we were hiding something in the closet. That bothered me some, but didn't keep me awake nights.

Now at Andrews and facing the prospect of a doctoral dissertation, I decided to tackle the doctrine of the sanctuary in the Adventist Church. It was a difficult decision for me to make, and I agonized over it for months. My hesitation came from not wanting to subject to any kind of scholarly analysis a subject that in my early days as an Adventist I'd found so utterly sublime. Eventually, however, I decided to go for it.

My ultimate intention was to do a theological study of the sanctuary doctrine itself, but I felt that that task should not be undertaken before I had a good handle on where the church had traveled on the issue. Hence the topic of my dissertation (since published): *The Sanctuary Doctrine: Three Approaches in the Seventh-day Adventist Church* (Berrien Springs, Michigan: Andrews University Press, 1981). I would study the perspectives of three prominent Adventist figures (Uriah Smith, Albion Fox Ballenger, and Milian L Andreasen), compare and contrast their positions in the light of Scripture and generally accepted Adventist beliefs, then come up with my own theological evaluation and assessment

But my research came into unexpectedly bold relief when, in the midst of it, what's come to be known as "the Desmond Ford crisis" broke.

Desmond Ford, an Adventist theologian from (church-owned) Avondale College in Australia, had gone on a teaching assignment to Pacific Union College in California. During a Sabbath afternoon forum while there, Ford made a presentation on the sanctuary that was so radical it sent shock waves all across the global Adventist community. The date was 1979, and I was in the middle of my research.

My own reaction after listening to a tape of the presentation was "Oh my dear, our doctrine of the sanctuary is finished. And here I am in the midst of writing a dissertation on it!"

Let me tell you, that's nightmare stuff! Writing a dissertation on an Adventist doctrine that's just been debunked? How does an Adventist minister grapple with a thing like that?

But something happened that to this day I find particularly intriguing and instructive. I secured a transcript of the presentation, and in the unhurried quietness of my own study read it carefully. And what I found was that my impression did a 180 degree turn. I discovered there was nothing of real substance there. Without meaning to be disrespectful in any way, I have to say that I found it 95% froth.

That surprised me, given my reaction to the audio. And the experience taught me something about charisma. If you ever encounter an argument or presentation that just about blows you away, even though it violates all that you had previously believed, get yourself a transcript of it. Then in the silence of your own home or office, study it carefully and see if, as a written document, it still makes the same impression. What sometimes happens, I think, is that the personality of the individual making a presentation can be so overpowering that it sweeps us completely off our feet and blinds us to problems and weaknesses in their position.

During those days, as I continued work on my dissertation, I disciplined myself to say nothing on the subject of the growing crisis in the church. I wanted calmness to come to my own conclusions. That's how we were taught to do research from my very early years under the British educational system. The idea was to pursue the evidence with complete dispassion, and to follow it wherever it led, regardless of the consequences. In addition to not commenting, I banned myself from reading anything from Ellen G. White's writings on the sanctuary theme. That's because I'd discovered in my preliminary research that one of the most frequent charges made by both Adventist and non-Adventist critics was that Seventh-day Adventists based their doctrine of the sanctuary on Ellen G. White's writings. So as I wrote my dissertation, one of my goals was to discover the biblical foundation of this teaching, independent of the writings of Ellen G White. I wanted my own assessment of the positions of these three Adventist thinkers to be based on the Bible alone.

Those were apprehensive days for me. I was bound by my conscience to follow the evidence wherever it led. And I had to grapple with the possibility, regardless of my assessment of the arguments of Desmond Ford, that the biblical evidence could well lead in a direction diametrically opposed to the position of these three men and the position of the church. What would I do then? My entire future as an Adventist minister could be at stake. It was that serious.

To shorten the story, I did finish the dissertation successfully.

Meanwhile, the General Conference had called together an international sanctuary review committee of scholars, pastors, administrators, and others to hear and assess the arguments of Desmond Ford. The committee met August 11-15, 1980, at the Glacier View Ranch, a church-owned retreat and conference center in the mountains near Boulder, Colorado. And through the influence of members of my dissertation committee, I was invited to attend and make a presentation of the findings of my work. As it turned out, the typing of my dissertation was completed in the early morning hours of August 11, the very day I left for Glacier View; and throughout the proceedings I remained in a state of apprehension, concerned that critical information and evidence might surface, that I had missed in my research. (Those were the days of typewriters, and no one wanted to face the nightmare of having to revise or revamp a chapter or two in the middle of a dissertation. Thankfully, that did not happen.)

In the end, the committee rejected the views of Dr. Ford and reaffirmed the basic Adventist positions on the sanctuary.

My dissertation was published, as indicated earlier—the first in the Andrews University dissertation series. And the (then) Southern Publishing Association expressed an interest in publishing what they called "a popular version" of it. Though I informally agreed to the proposal, an overseas seminary teaching assignment immediately

following my studies kept me fully occupied, leaving no time to pop-
ularize the work, as the publishers wanted. Besides, I shuddered at
the amount of work it would have taken to do that job well, and felt
a strong preference to plow new grounds, rather than re-work a field
already done. It was this desire to plow new ground that would land
me into my own controversy over the sanctuary doctrine, some 13
years after Glacier View.

While working on my dissertation, I'd made extensive notes and
collected reams of materials not relevant to the thesis. These I later
organized, brought together into a manuscript for a second book on
the sanctuary, and submitted it to the Review and Herald for publication. This was in 1993. As a general rule, before any book is published
by a church-owned publishing facility, it must get the approval of a
reading committee set up by the publishing house. (At least, that's
how it used to be). And when the subject is as sensitive as that of the
doctrine of the sanctuary (which lies at the center of Adventist faith),
then the reading committee is enlarged, as a safeguard.

The reactions from one or more members of the reading committee, passed on to me for my consideration as I prepared the final
draft of the manuscript, unnerved me. While writing my dissertation,
as I indicated above, I'd banned myself from reading or consulting
Mrs. White's writings on the sanctuary. And now that I was doing my
own theological assessment of the subject, it seemed to me that there
was all the more reason to follow the same approach, and I made
that clear in the introduction of the book (at the manuscript stage).
I wanted to see, I explained, whether the sanctuary doctrine is able
to stand on the Bible alone, independent of any Ellen White support,
notwithstanding the charges of critics to the contrary.

And although I did precisely that, I eventually dropped the explanation from the introduction because of the comment from one
reviewer. "[A] large portion of [Adventist readers]," this reviewer said,
"will see this . . . as tantamount to a disbelief in E.G.W."

I doubt there could be many Adventists more appreciative of the
writings of Ellen G. White than I am. I think they are a precious gift

that God, in His gracious providence, has given to us as a people. But I'm often struck by the misuse and abuse to which those writings are sometimes subjected. Ellen G. White herself admonished us to go back to the Bible; to substantiate our faith and belief from Scripture. At the last GC session she attended, she walked to the podium, held up her Bible, and said to the assembled delegates: "Brethren and Sisters, I commend unto you this Book" (reported by W. A. Spicer, then secretary of the GC, in *The Spirit of Prophecy in the Advent Movement*, p. 30; quoted in 6BIO 197.)

What I was doing in that 1993 book was to follow her counsel exactly. But somebody saw that as a bad idea. Well, I did it anyhow, but without explicitly disclosing the fact. (I should explain, however, that if you were to examine a copy of the book today, you will see an entire chapter dealing with the writings of Ellen G. White in respect to certain aspects of the doctrine of the sanctuary—as well as quotes from her writings here and there. But that chapter and those quotes came *after* the rest of the manuscript had been completed. My purpose for the inclusions was to preempt any attempts to use her writings to condemn or dismiss the case I was trying to build in the rest of the book.)

Here's another comment from a reviewer the publisher described as (quote) "a well-respected SDA scholar." "Adams," this person wrote, "implies there is no literal furniture in the heavenly sanctuary. I read [however] about all sorts of objects seen there in the book of Revelation." (So this person takes me to task for not advocating that there is "literal furniture in the heavenly sanctuary.") According to this same scholar–or probably another reviewer (I could not be sure, since no names were attached), "Adams ignores E.G.W.'s literal references to the heavenly sanctuary."

In another comment, a reviewer says: "Adams needs to preserve more physical movement on the part of God the Father and Christ in the heavenly sanctuary . . . ." So this person was interested in "more physical movement" in the heavenly sanctuary.

But the scariest comment of all was this one: "I hope I am wrong, but I can foresee a terrible firestorm of reaction to this book. I have not been so fearful about publishing a book in [all] my years of publishing work. Is Adams willing to go to another Glacier View meeting–this time with himself at the center of the discussion?"

Keep in mind that all these comments are coming to me while the book is in manuscript form. And I want to tell you, they get your attention! I felt that my whole future was on the line. After all, I have no uncles in the church. No father or brother in the church with big names or clout. I'm a first-generation Adventist. So I had to think seriously about it. Should I go forward, or should I pull back and not let the manuscript see the light of day?

I finally decided that honesty and integrity required that I move ahead. And, fortunately, the vast majority of the reading committee approved the document.

Some readers may wonder what sort of statements in the manuscript elicited such strong reactions. I would say that it was my interpretation of the heavenly sanctuary. Unfortunately, the book is now out of print, but you can probably find a copy in an Adventist library close to you. The title is *The Sanctuary: Understanding the Heart of Adventist Theology* (Hagerstown, MD: Review and Herald, 1993). What I tried to do in the book was to take the subject of the sanctuary, study it in all its facets, listen carefully to all the relevant questions about it—all the comments, observations, objections, criticisms; and then in the light of all the available evidence, formulate a position that is as watertight as I can possibly make it, and as solid as the biblical foundation on which the doctrine rests. Whatever I said about the sanctuary, I wanted people to be able to take that to the bank, so to speak—to have a sense that this is solid biblical stuff.

My ultimate conclusion was that in regard to the sanctuary doctrine, Adventists have not followed cunningly devised fables. The doctrine stands as solid as the rock on which it is planted. And that rock is Jesus Christ. Indeed, the doctrine is all about Him!

CHAPTER 10

On the Ground in Asia—Our Time in the Philippines

IT WAS FORTUITOUS (providential, in fact) that I should have been invited to attend the Glacier View meetings. In the months prior to my attendance there, the final period of my studies at Andrews University, the General Conference (GC) had forwarded a call to me from the Inter-American Division (IAD) to join the theology faculty of Montemorelos University in Mexico. The president of Montemorelos had visited me at Andrews, and things were being readied for my family's transfer to his campus.

Around January or February that year (1980), when we were both at Oakwood College (now Oakwood University) for speaking appointments, G. R. Thompson (by then secretary of the GC and a sleuth on church policy) had hinted to me that should I accept the call to Mexico, it could have important implications for my retirement service record. With retirement in those days extremely far away from my thinking, his words slid off my consciousness as water on a duck's back. I didn't get it. Now at Glacier, several months later, Thompson repeated his earlier warning in more pointed language. Should I go to Mexico, which is a part of the IAD (my home division), I'd be regarded as "a national returning." And because I'd not yet worked long enough in North America to become vested for retirement purposes (I had by then only worked about seven or eight years), it would mean that all my years in North America would be lost since, by church policy, they could not be added to my home division service credit.

Finally, I got it.

And with both the IAD president and the president of Montemorelos in attendance at the Glacier View meetings, I was able to sit down with both of them for a face-to-face personal explanation. Immediately sensing my predicament, they readily released me from the call, thereby giving the GC permission to pass on to me two other calls that they had frozen (because of the Inter-America possibility)—a call to River Plate College in Argentina and another to the Seventh-day Adventist Theological Seminary, Far East (now the Adventist International Institute of Advanced Studies, or AIIAS) near Manila in the Philippines. I quickly chose the Philippines out of language considerations. No one wants to be caught struggling with a new language (Spanish in the case of Argentina) while having to prepare brand new lectures in a host of subjects.

And Elder Thompson, to my everlasting gratitude, went even further. He shepherded a policy item leading to my adoption of North American as my home division, enabling me to travel to the Philippines with North America as my home base. How could I ever forget such extraordinary kindness! It marked the formal end of my "legal" connection to the IAD.

Now, with a new home base behind me, I headed out to Asia.

All the briefings at Missions Institute, notwithstanding, I remember our first reaction upon seeing Filipinos in large numbers. With our two young kids (Dwayne, 4 and Kim, 2)—Celia and I had flown from Orlando (where her Mom lived) to Atlanta, and then on to Los Angeles for a six-hour layover. We spent most of the time in the general area of the international terminal, with a variety of people occupying the scene. But as the time for our flight drew closer, we gravitated toward the departure gate, where Filipinos began to arrive—a few at first, then 30, then scores of them! Close to departure time, we were looking at something like 150 to 200, spread out in the waiting area.

And the thought that went through my mind was: *Oh, my dear, look at the number of them! And there'd be more where we're headed? What are we in for here?*

It was the beginning of what's usually called culture shock—our first experience. And it unnerved me. Now in retrospect, I cannot figure out what the concern in my head that day was all about. Filipinos turned out to be among the friendliest, most hospitable and welcoming groups of people I've ever met; and today, after living in their country with my family for six years, I feel almost as comfortable with them as I do with my own cultural group.

No one told me that I shouldn't have been dressed in jacket and tie upon arrival in the torrid Philippines capital of Manila. In the blazing heat and humidity, perspiration bathing down my face and neck, I found myself lugging a heavy carry-on, while holding 2-year old Kim in my arms, amidst the confusion and the crowd. A van from the seminary picked us up for the 50-minute trip to the campus.

The church-owned four-bedroom house at the top of the campus, where they located us, would be practically empty until our furniture and other household things arrived. My family loved the hilltop location, which gave us, from our backyard, a view of Laguna de Bay (literally, lake [of the town] of Bay—pronounced "by"), the largest lake in the Philippines, looking up at us in the distance. We would often close Sabbath sitting on our back steps, looking out over the lake, though it was not in the direction of the setting sun.

Our first instinct upon getting to our new home was to call our folks in the U.S. to inform them we'd arrived safely. But we quickly discovered there was no telephone in the house, none on the entire campus, nor any in the immediate surrounding villages. To make a call, we'd have to drive to Manila and have the telephone operator at our North Philippine Union office put through a call for us; alternatively, we could use a pay phone in the lobby at one of the major hotels in the city. The Inter-Continental Hotel in Makati (a section of greater Manila) was our favorite spot, offering us the greatest privacy.

It took weeks—months, in fact—for our shipment to arrive from the U.S., and some two or three pay periods for me to get onto the Far Easter Division (now the Southern Asia Pacific Division) payroll. And since I have an ingrained allergy to borrowing money or taking any "advance" from treasury, my family really had to do some serious scrimping, as the spending money we'd brought with us continued to dwindle. One way to cut expenses was to shop where the locals did—for fruits and vegetable, for rice and beans, and for other groceries. Early Friday mornings was the time a shopping bus left the campus with student families heading for the market in the town of Biñan, a forty-minute or so drive away. The bus leaves early, they told me, and in my mind I was thinking six-o'clock, six-thirty. But I shuddered when they gave me the exact departure time—4:00 a.m.! (Filipinos are very early risers—hence the prevalence of midday siestas.)

But if that was part of the price I had to pay for financial independence, so be it. In Biñan we shopped at huge, outdoor/indoor, farmers-style markets, with commodities priced at the local rate—in contrast to the much higher costs at the supermarkets in Manila that catered to the more affluent Filipinos, and frequented by expatriates. One learned a little of the art of "bargaining," a staple of Philippine shopping culture. When we arrived in the country, the currency exchange rate was 7.6 pesos to the U.S. dollar (today it's more than 43 pesos), and I very quickly made the mental switch to the new currency regime. I immediately began thinking in pesos, not calculating back to dollars to determine whether the price of an item was reasonable or not. Something was too expensive if I had to fork up too many pesos for it—it was that simple. And that mind-set served me well throughout our stay, even as the exchange rate drastically changed, falling to 20.5 pesos to the dollar by the time we left.

Before we owned a vehicle, I would walk to classes and to other appointments on the campus, with literally everything being down campus. I perspire easily, and it didn't take much to get me drenched. So imagine me purchasing a watermelon from the campus store and walking a quarter of a mile up the hill to my house in the blazing sun in the middle of the day, holding the huge fruit in one hand and a heavy briefcase in the other, with no hand free to wipe my sweating brow—and not wanting to put either load down before I got home! Eyes squinting from the salty sweat, my shirt soaking, I must have presented quite a sight! It was good that the iPhone with its ubiquitous camera had not yet been invented.

There was no air-conditioning, but once home on the hilltop, the breezes quickly cooled you down. From December to about March, the evenings were even chilly.

The Seminary, headed then by Dr. Leslie Hardinge and financed by the division, shared the same campus with Philippine Union College (now the Adventist University of the Philippines), headed by Dr. Alfonso Roda and financed by the North Philippine Union. And therein lay a long, complicated, and painful story—a most awkward history that, thankfully, lies outside the scope of this memoir. But one fundamental lesson it taught me was the peril of throwing together unevenly-financed "sisters" on the same grounds! It does not work well.

Even so, a few of the expats on campus worked for both institutions, Sam Robinson being one of them—in charge, as I remember it, of campus projects and operations. Not long after we arrived, Sam worked out an auto deal for us with one of his friends in Manila—for a huge, black Chevrolet, more than a decade old at the time. The price was good. But that first day, as I drove through the campus gate with it, it literally brought the ballgame in the nearby field to a complete stop. In a country where most cars are small to midsize, many students had never seen a sight like that. Suddenly I became the object of an entire field of gawkers; and in my mind I imagined going around the country and being identified as "that big Black American guy in the big black American Chevrolet." Not exactly the image I wanted to create.

Within three days, the vehicle was back outside its owner's house in Manila, an outcome made easier by the fact that no money had yet changed hands.

My second vehicle was a small 6-year-old (4 cylinder) Ford Escort, which I used that first April in the country to take my family to our first vacation in the Philippines—to the mountain resort of Baguio (which we'd heard about during our mission institute orientation). Anyone who's ever traveled to that popular destination knows that getting there is not a piece of cake, but involves navigating a long, narrow, winding mountain road, with the gradient getting steeper with every meter. Half-way up the mountain, on a steep incline, our engine lost all power, with the foot and hand brakes together hardly able to keep the vehicle from sliding backwards. It all scared the daylights out of our daughter Kim, and she began crying in panic. It was not a pleasant situation.

Perhaps I should spare you the horrible details, including how Celia had to get out and jam a couple of large rocks behind the back wheels so we wouldn't roll back into a culvert right behind us, large enough to accommodate the entire back side of our vehicle. Fortunately, we were on the "safe" side of the road, the side that hugged the mountain, but it was still a frightening affair. (Overheating was the problem, and the vehicle started up again after we'd raised the hood and allowed it to cool for a while). Driving their own vehicle, Graduate school professor, Dr. Hedrick Edwards (from Trinidad and Tobago), his wife Lenoa, and their two young children were on the trip with us, accompanied by Seminary-Graduate School librarian Janet Miller. It was a comfort to have them there for help and support. They'd been longer in the country and were more familiar with the lay of the land.

Finally, we managed to come to the last major climb before entering Baguio. It was then that the Escort, as if taking on a mind of its own, refused to go any further. It was a section of road about 100 yards (91 meters) long—rising almost perpendicular (I'm exaggerating only slightly) in front of you. Our first three tries ended the same way—we'd get about a third of the way up, and the car would lose engine power to go forward. Putting the vehicle in neutral and with foot heavy on the brakes, we'd let it roll back down to a broad staging area, as I ended up calling it.

Eventually, we figured out that that segment of road was not five or six lanes wide for no reason. Those who'd built it had wisely anticipated just the kind of problem I was having, and had created the broad, level asphalted staging area as a safe fallback—a place where the frazzled driver could pause and reconsider their approach. And the idea (which we got from a kind traveler from Cavite, not far from our campus) was not to proceed straight up, as we'd been trying to do, but to advance in a winding, zigzag pattern, drastically lessening the engine thrust needed for the climb. Doing that, we finally made it into Baguio, and had a good time up in mountain resort.

But a few weeks later, on a Sunday morning, the Escort burned to the ground just about 20 yards from our home, shortly after I'd left the house to run an errand down campus. Providentially, the incident did not happen during that Baguio trip, or in the middle of Manila traffic, or in any other way that would have put my family or others in danger!

Starting out as an assistant professor (I would become a full professor before leaving the Philippines), I was operating sometimes just one lesson ahead of my students. It demanded hours and hours of preparation (that first year, especially) developing new lectures in the seven areas of theology I taught—anthropology, soteriology, eschatology, etc. Our students hailed from the Philippines, Indonesia, Singapore, Malaysia, India, Bangladesh, South Korea, Japan, Thailand, and other Asian countries. There also were students from Africa, Europe, the Caribbean, and the United States. An international student body, as was the faculty.

In addition, the seminary conducted extension schools on location; and I had opportunity to conduct classes throughout the region—in Japan, South Korea, Indonesia, and Bangladesh; as well as seminars and speaking appointments in Singapore, Hong Kong, Taiwan, and elsewhere.

Teaching seminary was stimulating work in a number of ways, providing endless opportunities for interaction and learning—learning from the Philippines itself (with its colorful traditions and people), from the various cultures present on the campus, from the local faculty and staff, and from fellow expatriate colleagues and their families.

Campus life was quiet. We had radios, but no telephones (as mentioned before) and no television. After a few years, a television set appeared on campus—in the home of the then current seminary president, Dr. Werner Vyhmeister, with the ability to pick up two or three local stations. Some Saturday nights saw a lyceum of some kind; but most times people created their own entertainment. My family would often walk down campus, meeting and talking to students and other faculty along the way. Once I made it onto the division's payroll, my family would take an almost weekly trip to Manila—to conduct business at the bank; to shop for clothing, for groceries, etc.); to call home; to get service on our vehicle; and so forth. Sometimes the kids came with us, other times we left them at home with our house helper.

A dangerous situation developed one day early into our stay. I'd gone alone to Manila for repairs on my vehicle. I'd been told the car would be ready by 2:00 p.m. But when two o'clock turned into four, and four into five, with nothing to show for it, I decided it was time to head back to campus by public transportation. It was a decision that called for some round-about maneuvers in a huge city still largely unfamiliar to me, until I could find a jeepney to take me to Balibago, a town about eight miles or so from the campus. In my ignorance as a newcomer to the country, I thought that from Balibago I would simply catch another jeepney going up the Balibago Road that runs by the campus. In fact, that was indeed one of the usual ways to reach the campus. But what I didn't know was that by 6:30 p.m. (after dark in the Philippines), those jeepneys stopped running the route from Balibago past the campus.

So I arrived in the town, only to discover that I had no way of getting home that time of the evening. After asking around for about 45 minutes, I realized I was stranded. Not a policeman in sight or any other apparent authority figure. And even finding someone who spoke any English was difficult. As I went back and forth, desperate,

I ran into a Roman Catholic priest, who graciously offered to put me up at his church for the night. But I had to decline his kind gesture, since I knew that my wife would be frantic with worry, having no idea where I was, there being no means of alerting her concerning my whereabouts.

About an hour and a half after arriving in the town, that same priest helped me negotiate a special ride to the campus. A man with a jeepney would take me for 50 pesos (about 16 times the daytime rate). But given my predicament, I grabbed on to the deal, even though I could tell that the driver, who could speak a little English, had been drinking. Filipinos hardly do anything alone and, true to custom, this driver took along with him three "companions" (a typical Filipino expression), one in the passenger seat beside him, and the other two, both drunk, at the back of the jeepney with me.

The road from Balibago to the campus, commonly regarded by those of us on campus as the worst road in the Philippines for pot-holes, is a lonely one that time of night, passing through desolate, (non-residential) cane fields. And it was not hard for me to imagine that mischief could easily befall me at any time during the 20-minute ride. Especially did that seem a possibility when one of the men in the back with me pulled out a knife, its shiny blade catching my eyes in the darkness. "Don't worry," said the driver, hearing me ask the guy what he was doing, "he wouldn't hurt you."

Cold comfort, I thought, breathing a silent prayer, and preparing for a quick dispatch of the staggering two-some in the back with me, should it come to that. (I was too preoccupied with watching the two at the back with me to bother about how I'd handle the other two at the front afterwards.)

What a huge relief when they finally—finally—pulled up in front of my home on campus! Relief for me, but equally (if not more so) for my wife and kids who, by that time, were almost hysterical with fear for my safety. It would be quite a while before the two search-teams of expat men would arrive back on campus. One team had gone up the Tagaitay road (an extension of the Balibago road in the opposite direction from the one I was on) and the other, after a quarter mile down the Balibago Road, had turned right onto another road through the cane fields, just in case I'd run into trouble there. But they were all looking to spot my vehicle, and never would have suspected I was traveling by jeepney. They too were immensely relieved to learn, upon returning, that I'd made it back safely.

Following that incident, Sam Robinson purchased two-way radios from Japan for all of the expat men, helping us to keep in constant communication with someone on campus (selected for that particular day) while we were heading home from Manila or elsewhere—whether after sunset or during daylight. We all took on code names. Mine was "Rabbit."

Wearing Four Hats at Once

As the General Conference session convened in 1985, the president of the seminary left to serve as a delegate to the session, with furlough immediately following. The business manager (and one or two other expat workers) also left on furlough. And thus it was that yours truly found himself simultaneously wearing four hats at once—holding the offices of theology professor (my main job), chair of the international school board, acting business manager of the seminary, and acting president of the seminary.

Try getting your head around that for a minute!

My first morning on the jobs in the seminary found me somewhat in a quandary as to which of my three offices to occupy first. Eventually, since the business manager's was the closest as I would enter the complex, I sat there first. Within minutes a woman showed up and requested to see me. Her husband was an overseas seminary student, and she'd come to report that their vehicle had been stolen overnight.

The first thing that came to mind to say to her was: *Why not report this to the president?* Then just as quickly I remembered that *I was also the president.* So after questioning her about the details of her story, we set out in my car, accompanied by the registrar, to file a report at the nearest police station—in the town of Tagaytay, about 20 minutes away.

The police chief, away from his office when we arrived, eventually walked in, wearing civilian shorts and flip-flops. But within seconds after we sat down together, he'd put his finger on the single detail we wanted most to avoid: "Was the car registered?"

Questioning the student's wife earlier, I'd learned that they'd just acquired the vehicle and were currently in the process of registering it; and to this day I'm amazed that the casual-looking officer could get so quickly to this central issue. It took a lot of dancing around to avoid a direct answer to that pivotal question. In the end, having no transportation of his own at the station (a strange situation, to say the least), the chief suggested I drive him to Puting Kahoy (the village nearest the campus, where he suspected the thief came from), so he might conduct an investigation of the theft.

This I diplomatically declined to do, not wanting my personal vehicle associated with a police investigation. After all, it was the same vehicle I would have to use to drive through that very neighborhood on almost a weekly basis.

How the case eventually was resolved I cannot now remember. But it was certainly a chilling start to my first day in the dual role of business manager-president.

Experiences on the Road

Members of the seminary faculty often traveled to various Asian countries for speaking appointments and extension schools, and I took my turn, with special experiences coming not only from the classroom, but also on the road.

Such was the case on my way to Manado on the island of Sulawesi in Indonesia for an extension school. I became stranded in Ujung Pandang on the southern tip of the island of Sulawesi, after the plane developed engine trouble. I remember my predicament when I couldn't find a single person who spoke sufficient English to help me alert my hosts in Manado about my situation. Somehow or other, I did manage to solve the messy problem; but it was a stark reminder that English is not as universal as it's often cracked up to be.

In another experience, I arrived in Taiwan for a series of speaking appointments as thirsty as a dog stranded in the Sahara. With no bottled water available (for some reason), I proceeded to boil tap water and try to cool it down in the freezer section of the refrigerator in the little apartment where they were housing me. When you're almost completely dehydrated, and facing a speaking appointment in 90 minutes, that's when you discover that neither soft drinks nor hot water quenches thirst; and that's when you realize how long it takes boiling water to cool, even when placed in a freezer. At one point I thought I was going stark mad. It's one of the most unpleasant experiences imaginable to begin speaking with one's throat as dry as dust, and with no potable water available. (Usually, there was an abundance of bottled water almost everywhere I traveled, and I cannot for the life of me remember now what made that occasion different.)

Another travel memory came during a stopover in Germany on my way home on furlough in 1983. My family had gone ahead to Orlando, but I made the roundabout jaunt in an effort to pick up a few scraps of German at the famous Goethe Institute in Lüneburg. Heading into the city the day after arriving, I discovered how necessity can force one to "get" the prevailing language in a big hurry. As best I could, I tried to signal to the gentleman sitting by me in the bus that I didn't speak German. But not taking no for an answer (or perhaps not understanding the extent of my ignorance), he proceeded to talk with me in German all the way into town. And what I found strange (even to this very day) is that I was able to glean key bits of information from him—such as, for example, the location of the office to reconfirm my outgoing flight; and that he considered Seventh-day Adventists a cult (although I cannot now remember how we managed to get to that second item).

On my last Sabbath in Germany I attended a vesper service in Berlin and was surprised I was able to follow the entire sermon, a huge contrast to my first Sabbath in the country, when I became bored to death during the all-German Sabbath school lesson study. (I think I preached that day, and so was able to, at least, follow the sermon).

Back in Orlando, I found myself wanting to respond in German as my folks talked to me. But within a week to ten days, it was all gone; and it hasn't come back since, notwithstanding the occasional efforts by Klaus and Irmi Ruh (longtime German friends of mine, at whose home I stayed while there) to revive the smattering of the language that had remained.

It was a good furlough...traveling to our various stops in the U.S. and Canada by American Airlines on a special, low-rate deal they had for tickets purchased overseas. Those were the days when U.S. airlines would serve a meal on domestic flights; and under the travel arrangements we had, we got to see (I didn't say "eat") the same food again and again and again

Returning to the Philippines with jet lag, and plunging immediately into classes, I was sure that I sometimes would fall asleep for split seconds in the middle of those first lectures. (Thankfully, none of the students ever pointed that out, and I keep hoping they never noticed.)

In the Midst of Political Crisis

We arrived in the Philippines during the time of President Ferdinand Marcos and his colorful (and powerful) wife Imelda. But before we left, they would be gone, chased out of the country amid the political crisis following the elections of February 7, 1986. The so-called "snap elections" (for president and vice president only) had been called to mark the end of Marshall Law in the country, and pitted President Marcos against Cory Aquino for the presidency. Aquino was the widow of opposition leader Benigno (Ninoy) Aquino, Jr., who'd been killed on the tarmac of the Manila Airport as he arrived from a three-year self-exile in United States. The fact that he was killed while in the custody of a Philippine military escort naturally led to the suspicion that the government was somehow complicit in his murder, which heightened domestic and international political pressure on the Marcos regime.

Those elections, partly an attempt by Marcos to quiet critics, backfired badly. According to one source, "vote-buying, strong-arm tactics, and other forms of naked electoral violations marked the voting, not only in the remote areas controlled by political warlords, but in the very heart of Manila, before the eyes of news correspondents and foreign observers" (*People Power: The Philippine Revolution of 1986*, p. 67). All this notwithstanding, it was clear, as the vote tallies continued, that Aquino was winning.

That could not be allowed to happen, and the commission on election (responsible for the vote count) began delaying tactics, leading at one point to a dramatic walkout of young computer workers from the election commission office in Manila (as the pro-Marcos parliament readied itself to intervene and declare in favor of Marcos), all the evidence to the contrary notwithstanding (*People Power*, p. 67).

The elections took place on a Friday, making the following Sabbath one of the most difficult I ever had to keep. Like every single soul in the country, I wanted to know the outcome of the vote; and with the radio the only source of information in our house, I had it set to record during the Sabbath hours. It was tuned to Radio Veritas, a Catholic station in Manila, widely regarded as the only source of un-doctored political news. With the volume turned to zero, all I had to do was release the pause button when my watch alarm indicated it was time for a major news broadcast. This meant I could catch up on all the election developments after sunset.

Perhaps you can see how that arrangement, however sanitized to respect the Sabbath, would nevertheless intrude upon the sacred hours; because each time my watch alarmed, it deflected my mind from the sacred day to something perhaps alien to it. The only mitigating factor—and one on which I leaned heavily in self-justification, was the recognition that something of dire consequence was taking place in the country—a premonition that, at least, turned out to be correct.

What I discovered, however—and what I've found to be true

in numerous other cases where some important news story seems poised to break over the Sabbath hours—was that *nothing significant* had taken place during Sabbath, after all; and that I needn't have bothered. No results had been announced that day, none the day after, and none during all the following week. By the middle of the second week with no announcement of the election results, tensions in the country had mounted to dangerous levels, the general belief being that President Marcos and his people, having clearly lost, were busily cooking the books.

As documented incidences of fraud continued to grow, prominent domestic and international entities issued statements of condemnation. "This chain of events eventually led to the resignation of Marcos' Defense Minister Juan Ponce Enrile, and Armed Forces Vice-Chief of Staff General Fidel Ramos. Enrile and Ramos then secluded themselves in the military and police headquarters of Camp Aguinaldo and Camp Crame, respectively, leading to [what's come to be known as] the People Power Revolution from February 22-25, 1986, which dismantled the Marcos regime" ("Philippine Presidential Elections, 1986," *Wikipedia.*)

Those were tense days for the Philippines. I remember driving into Manila on February 25 (against the advice of the seminary president) to conduct a funeral. It was on the very day that the country saw two rival presidents sworn in—Marcos at a heavily guarded presidential palace, and Aquino at Club Filipino in Greenhills, Metro Manila. Dr. Esmeraldo De Leon (a faculty colleague) was with me and, surprisingly, we found a Manila that was the quietest I'd ever seen it—traffic-wise and otherwise. Contingency evacuation plans had been laid by the American embassy for U.S. and Canadian nationals, plans that, thankfully, it never had to execute—although, to tell the truth, I'd been half looking forward to the excitement, never having been evacuated from anywhere before. (Silly, isn't it?)

Months later, in October 1986, my family and I were heading back to Canada. Our term had ended, and I'd been called by the Seventh-day Adventist Church in Canada (the Canadian Union) to be the associate secretary of the union and editor of the *Canadian Adventist Messenger*. It was on the eve of that departure that something happened that I've always looked back on with the deepest regret.

A Stressful Ending

Among the many things that had to be done before leaving was getting rid of our vehicle. After returning the big black Chevrolet (mentioned earlier) to its original owner, and after the Ford Escort burned, we'd procured a used Opal Ascona. Knowing we were about to leave, the new business manager for the seminary, Pastor Daniel Nestares from Argentina, offered us 85,000 pesos for the vehicle (about $4250.00, US). While thinking about the offer, I just happened to be jogging early one morning with a fellow expat, who was also leaving. Amid all the huffing and puffing as we jogged, he told me what a good price he was getting for his vehicle (a better one than mine, admittedly) on the open market in Manila.

That bit of intelligence put an idea into my head that proved disastrous in the end. Declining the business manager's offer, I instead put the car on the open market in Manila, with small classified ads in the local papers there. It was a process that ended up consuming a vast amount of my time, what with having to make the car available for hood-lifting and tire-kicking; or leaving it on display at the union compound, etc. It was a worry that I needed as much as I did a hole in the head in those busy, hectic days before our departure, with a hundred and one items on my plate. Nightmare, that's what it was.

And as if that was not enough, something else entered to complicate the picture. Here's what happened.

Ever since we arrived in the Philippines, I'd been meaning to take my family to Corregidor, the historic island of World War II fame at the entrance to Manila Bay. A military base, the island suffered heavy bombardment toward the end of the war, with many American, Filipino, and Japanese soldiers losing their lives there. It's one of the most important historic landmarks of the war in the Asian theater, a must-see for anyone claiming to have lived in the Manila area for any length of time. But every time I thought of the cost of the trip there— something like US $14.00 a head, it seemed too much for this missionary's budget, when multiplied by four and calculated into pesos.

But on the eve of our permanent departure from the country, I returned from appointments in Japan and Bangladesh to exciting news from my wife. She'd heard that there was to be an Adventist excursion to Corregidor that coming Sunday, for something like seven pesos a head! It was just the deal I'd been waiting for, and I immediately set to work to secure four tickets. Never mind we had just two weeks left in the country, an offer like that seemed just too good to pass up.

About 3000 Adventists all around the Manila area and the campus where we lived also thought it was a good deal, and descended on the docks that Sunday morning. The carrier was a huge warship of World War II vintage that had seen better days. And it took about an hour and a half to get us all on board through a single, narrow gangplank. It was a nice day as we took off for the two-hour ride to the place, folks having fun and enjoying the fellowship.

But a typhoon was moving through the area, and by the time we arrived on the island, its front had begun to pour rain down on us. There was hardly any shelter on the open deck, and the few people with umbrellas did their best to help family and friends. We made it to Corregidor about midday, and some of us took the tour of the military ruins—old barracks, abandoned canons, caves, and so forth. But the intermittent rain killed off the sightseeing spirit, and by about 2:00 o'clock hundreds of us were ready to get back to Manila. But it took until about 4:00 to ensure that everyone had made it back on board, and by that time we were into low tide, with the ship wedged into rocks. When the captain tried to push off, the engine shut down, and we were stranded.

Four o'clock turned into five o'clock; into six o'clock; then seven. By 10, everyone knew we were in for something bad. The small crew worked through the night to no avail. It was a rotten situation. Some families were lucky to find shelter for their women and children in a house up the little hill on the island, where they slept sardine-like on the concrete floor. But most of us remained on the ship, the majority of us abandoning the rain-soaked, open deck for the belly of the boat, where, unfortunately, water was collecting. There was no place to lie down, and hardly any dry spot to even sit down. It was a horrible night. Celia and I found a place where just one of the kids could sit down on coils of rope and lean back a little. So we had them take turns during the night, about an hour at a time, while we remained standing, or sometimes literally leaning on each other for balance while sitting precariously on a plank or something. It was sheer misery.

Moreover, there were no toilet facilities aboard the ship and none on shore. So you can try to imagine our situation as Monday morning came, with no budge from the engine. By that time we were all starving, of course. My family had expected to be home in time for supper Sunday night, and so we'd packed only a light snack for the day, thinking we'd be able to buy something to eat on the road, if necessary. But with thousands of hungry souls landing on its doorstep, the small grocery shop/eatery on the island was completely overwhelmed in no time, its emptied shelves staring hungry shoppers in the face.

Late Monday morning, Celia found two granola bars in her purse, and had our two kids share one between them. The other was for her and me. But how could we eat it by ourselves while the German visitor we'd been talking to had nothing? So we divided the bar in three and offered him a piece … and he took it! We were all that hungry!

By Monday afternoon, the typhoon that had moved through Manila, leaving flooded streets in its wake, had begun to hit Corregidor with pelting rain; and the ship's engine situation had not changed. Only my wife and I knew how utterly frustrated we were, with a million things still to do in preparation for our departure, now less than 10 days away. And we had a car to sell.

As Monday rolled on and the feeling of being utterly stuck and helpless grew on us, I briefly entertained the thought of hiring one of the small fishing boats docked nearby to take my family back across the 30 miles (48 kms) of water to Manila. But in that kind of weather, you don't fool with Manila Bay and, in retrospect, I'm glad we didn't take that risk.

By whatever signal, word of our predicament somehow managed to get to Manila, and we all rejoiced to see a second ship headed our way as Monday was ending. We rejoiced even more to learn that it had come for us. It was smaller, and it took hours to finish the passenger transfer amid the turbulence. But all eventually made it safely on board, where, thankfully, we could go into the belly of the ship and away from the rain. Moreover, the crew of that second ship graciously offered a bowl of steamed white rice to parents with children. Severely rationed, a single bowl had to do for Kim and Dwayne. With growling stomachs, we watched them eat the small morsel, full knowing it would do very little for their empty stomachs and, of course, nothing for ours.

The departure of that second ship was a prolonged affair, to say the least; and it was heading toward ten o'clock by the time we docked at the pier back in Manila. Every family wanted to be the first to get off, of course; and the rush toward the exit came close to tipping the vessel, leading to frantic announcements for hundreds of passengers to back away from the dockside, so as to balance the ship.

Further delaying our evacuation was the fact that, with the high tide, the gangplank was too short to reach the dock, ending more than four feet above it. This meant that some folk (children and the elderly, especially) had to be lifted down for the final landing. Some soft padding or mattress was put in place so younger passengers could make a jump for it. With the ship rocking all the while in the choppy seas, it made every move down the gangway perilous, and we were fortunate that we lost no one, nor suffered any injury. It took close to two hours, if you can believe it, for passengers to disembark via that single, narrow gangway.

A large, anxious group was waiting on shore, relieved to see us after being terrified by rumors the first vessel had sunk in the typhoon, and many of us had perished. And it was a relief to see ADRA

Philippines on the scene with food and dry clothing. But getting into waiting buses was quite another story in itself.

To cut it short, instead of arriving home Sunday evening, as we'd planed, my family got back about two o'clock Tuesday morning—tired, dirty, and extremely frustrated. For the next few days we became a (good-natured) laughing stock for those who'd not fallen for the excursion deal. But that didn't faze us; we were only thankful to make it out alive—and safe.

In our case, safe but extremely frustrated. We'd lost valuable time. We'd practically blown three solid days. Now I was left regretting that I'd not paid the fourteen dollars a head and taken the trip years earlier, using one of those comfortable, swift-moving hydrofoils that ferried tourists to and from the island.

With much time lost, we abandoned all hopes of selling the car before our departure. There was no buyer, and we were forced to leave the vehicle in the care of a local gentleman we considered very spiritual and trustworthy. He would handle the sale, keep a small commission, and forward the rest to us. It turned out to be a long, protracted, and frustrating process that stretched across nine months!

As the weeks went by, with us trying vainly to contact this person from the U.S. and from Canada, we eventually turned to the business manager of the seminary, Pastor Nestares, for help—the very one who'd at the beginning offered us 84,000 pesos for the car. His heavy load notwithstanding, he gave us valuable assistance that finally brought the matter to a conclusion, the brother in question remitting through Nestares what he said was the cost of the vehicle—about 34,000 pesos. Had we accepted Nestares' offer, it would have saved us tons of heartache and anxiety. Now, to my keen embarrassment, he had to be the one to forward me the proceeds of the sale—an amount far below what he was prepared to pay about a year earlier. So we lost 50,000 pesos on the deal.

But however painful, it was not the end of the world. We got over it, and moved on.

Saying Goodbye

Apart from the customary farewells, the days before departure were occupied with packing and shipping household stuff, selling some things, and giving away a whole lot—to local friends and "helpers" in our home. The specifics of all that have faded in memory now, except this one: When I gave my hammer to the guy whose job it was to repair and fix broken things in homes around the campus—particularly in expat homes—he paused in silence for what felt like thirty seconds; then he said wistfully: "Now I own an American hammer!" It just about blew me away—for here I thought I was doing just a little, insignificant thing.

My family and I bonded well with Filipinos, and there remains a deep affection in our hearts for that country and its colorful, friendly people. Locals stared at us, to be sure—especially at first. We were different. But throughout our stay the people we met afforded us all the respect and honor anyone could expect—nothing short. Today I feel at home with them wherever they come together in the United States. And whenever the occasion warrants, I wear the Barong Tagalog proudly.

CHAPTER **11**

Back to Canada... and On to the General Conference

THE ADVENTIST CHURCH has promoted foreign mission for some 140 years. But the church often falls short when it comes to its support and re-establishment of returning missionaries. Not infrequently (in the cases of those returning to the North American Division), their names are placed on a list circulated to unions, conferences, and educational institutions, publicizing their availability. But often, with employing entities running on full complement and tight budgets, many returning workers are left to languish, or forced to accept jobs not entirely in their field of competence.

Fortunately for me—and without my asking—a call came through from the Seventh-day Adventist Church in Canada (the Canadian Union) precisely at the right time—to become associate secretary of the union.

Though Orlando was our home base during my family's stay in the Philippines, Canada had been our residence before embarking on post-graduate studies and subsequently accepting the call to Asia. Both Celia and I had gone to school in Canada, and had both lived and worked there. Thus it was like returning home for us. Our kids enrolled at the Adventist elementary school at the back of Kingsway College, and Celia worked with the public health services of Ontario.

Though born in the U.S., our children were very young when we left Andrews University for the Philippines; and thus the first country they identified with in North America was Canada. (When later we moved back to the U.S., we could tell that that identity was fading when they began rooting for American teams over those from Canada. It took some years, but it did happen—though I sense they still have a soft spot for the north country.)

As associate secretary of the union, I no longer had to set and administer exams—as I did when I was a seminary professor; did not have to prepare and deliver lectures four days a week; and I did not have to read term papers! But I missed the interaction with students, the give-and-take of ideas in the classroom, and the friendly banter when class was over and I didn't have another one immediately following.

But as associate secretary, I had the privilege of working closely with the secretary, Glen Maxson, the very one who years earlier had made that memorable appeal following his sermon at the Port of Spain youth congress mentioned above in a previous chapter. He could never have imagined that, years later, a certain young man who'd doggedly sat through his call that day would be working with him side by side as his associate, thousands of miles from the venue of that morning's service. Nor would that young man have pictured this in his wildest dreams. But here we were, thrown together in the same office.

Three memories come to mind during my time as associate secretary.

The first has to do with the Fax machine—of all things. I believe it was the end of 1986 (or perhaps the beginning of 1987). The union had scheduled one of its committee meetings in Halifax, Nova Scotia (in the dead of winter), and the big agenda item one morning was a demonstration of the capability of the telefax technology just then coming into vogue. At a pre-determined time, we all gathered around the Fax machine we'd taken with us; and we were told that someone back at headquarters in Oshawa, 760 miles away, would write a note to us, feed it through the office Fax unit and phone line, and that that note would mysteriously emerge in front of us on our machine there in Halifax.

Just describing the process brings an awkward feeling—a feeling of ancientness. But back then it left us all with mouths wide open to actually see it happen. And it must bring a chuckle to many younger people reading these lines to imagine that the Fax machine, confined to only specialized uses today, could have been such a big deal less than 30 years ago.

The second memory goes back to the election of a president for the Quebec Conference (the former Ontario-Quebec Conference having been split into two separate entities). I believe the date was sometime in mid-1987; and Dr. Robert Samms, then living in New York (but who previously had pastored the largest church in Quebec), was considered a prime candidate. In the lead-up to the union committee meeting in Winnipeg, Manitoba, with the election of a president for Quebec a top item on its agenda, three of us from the union office—Doug Devenich (from Public Affairs and Religious Liberty), Lawton Lowe (from Ministerial), and I met with Samms in a hotel lobby near the Toronto airport. We wanted to feel him out on his willingness to accept the job, if it were offered; and he'd flown up to Toronto, at our invitation and expense, to meet with us. We reported back to union president Jim Wilson on Samms' willingness to come, if invited; and so Wilson brought the item to the committee.

As the discussion proceeded, with unexpected opposition from some quarters, a lay member of the committee (a brother of east Asian background, I believe) suggested that since some members of the committee did not know the candidate, we should probably do a video interview with him, and bring it to the next committee meeting (in three months or so).

I can't tell you the number of times I've seen a Caucasian candidate voted into office following anecdotal testimonials, such as: "I know him; he's a good man; he has a lovely wife and great kids." But then comes a black candidate (as Samms was), and this brother has the temerity to call for a videotape interview! I was literally ready to explode.

Fortunately—for me perhaps—the chairman brushed aside the awkward suggestion. "That won't be necessary," Wilson said. "I think enough of us know Pastor Samms to make a decision." I simmered down. The name was voted.

The third memory came in early June of 1988 when, in the wake of Glen Maxson's retirement, the union committee met to elect his replacement. I had no big desire to succeed Maxson, but in our system (and I'm speaking purely in terms of administrative protocol and precedent), that would have seemed the obvious (and decent) thing that should happen. And, speaking frankly, I suspected that if the associate secretary had been Caucasian, there'd have been no contest.

But the facts being what they were, several candidates suddenly appeared upon the scene, ready to take the job. One conference president, taking me aside, confided what was being said about me by some of his colleagues. "They're saying that you don't listen," he told me—a charge that literally floored me. And I began to reflect on why, in the humble station of associate secretary, I needed to "listen" to anyone. After all, I couldn't remember anyone bringing their troubles or issues to me! Why would they?

In this case, they couldn't say they didn't know me and so demand to see a video; but, lacking that, any old excuse would do. "They're saying," the conference president also told me, "that they'd prefer a son of the soil for the job"—and I immediately understood the meaning of those coded words. And so a native son was elected.

On June 29, about three weeks after the vote, I headed for a camp meeting appointment in North New South Wales, Australia; and before I could return to Canada, the General Conference (GC) came calling—for me to join the *Adventist Review* staff as associate editor.

I was told by a member that as my name came up before the GC administrative committee, one committee member held out for a while against it, charging I'd written for *Spectrum* magazine, which at that time was making huge waves in some sectors of the

Adventist Church. (This, incidentally, was not the case. I'd not written for *Spectrum*, unless one should count a letter to the editor as "writing for" the journal. And in the letter, as I recall, I was actually taking issue with a particular article that had appeared in the magazine. But supposing I'd actually "written for" *Spectrum*, just the idea that someone would have held *that* against me, regardless of *what* I'd written! The narrowness we have in some sectors of the church is astonishing.)

The developments surrounding the union secretary's position made it easy for me to say yes to the GC, and avoid the awkwardness of having to provide on-the-job training for the new secretary. (I should mention here that the new secretary, so far as I knew, was not one of those anxious for the job. Moreover, he and I had worked well together, collaborating on several church projects and issues on our own.)

My affirmative response to the GC set in motion a whirlwind of activities in preparation for the move to the Washington D.C. area. It involved, among other things, traveling to Washington to enroll our kids in the local Adventist school; contacting a real estate agent to look for a place to stay; setting up a bank account; sitting down with GC treasury about a home mortgage; etc.

With Adventist schools in the Washington area set to commence near the end of August, there was no time to lose; and I set out with the family early on Sunday August 21, heading for Washington. They would take up temporary residence in GC housing, while work on our new house was completing and while I packed our things and finished up my work at the union office.

We entered the U.S. in Celia's Buick Skylark, a vehicle that fully complied with U.S. emissions standards. Leaving the Skylark with her, I flew back to Oshawa, and to my 1986 Pontiac, whose flashy dashboard had sold the car to me. I just loved how it lit up in the dark! But when, several weeks after returning—and days before I was to leave for the U.S.—I had it tested for compliance with U.S. emissions regulations, it failed, badly. They told me at the General Motors dealership there in Oshawa that it would cost me about $1600.00 to bring it in compliance.

The news left me utterly discouraged and devastated. With my wife and kids already in the U.S., I remember going back to the empty house at 314 Labrador Drive feeling dejected. On a whim I turned on the television, and at that precise moment, they began playing Bobby McFerrin's song (released that very month—September 1988), "Don't Worry, Be Happy," with all its animation and antics. My first instinct was to change the channel or turn the silly thing off—I didn't need someone mocking me, not at that time. I needed time to worry and fret over my miserable predicament. But something about the piece kept me from changing the channel or pressing the off button. Halfway through the song, I broke into a smile; and I was actually chuckling when, toward the end, it came to the line that said: "Don't worry, don't do it, be happy. Put a smile on your face."

Does God have a sense of humor or what?

I knew I couldn't afford the emissions fix; and so, two days after the moving truck left with our things, I headed for the border with the Pontiac, hoping against hope. At customs they checked the serial number and, sure enough, found the vehicle in non-compliance. I cannot be allowed into the U.S. on a permanent basis with it.

If you've never been through a situation like that, then you probably did not catch the gravity of the predicament I just described. I no longer had a family in Canada; no longer had a home in Canada; or a bank account; or any belongings; or a job. And here I was at the U.S. border being turned back to Canada. With a heart heavier than half a sack of led, I went back to the car, ready to turn around and head over the bridge back into Windsor. I'm sure I was praying, but it was the kind of prayer too deep for words. And moments after turning on the ignition, I shut it down, suddenly remembering that the immigration officer had forgotten to return my driver's license to me.

As I'm heading back into the building to retrieve it, a thought comes into my mind (placed there by Divine Providence, I believe), and I proceed to share it with the agent: "Sir," I said, "my car is completely packed and my family is already in the U.S. Why not let me enter the country without technically 'landing' the vehicle; then return to Canada and work on the emissions issue?"

From his reaction, I could tell that a light had gone on in his head. Pondering the idea, he walked away to consult with a superior. And after what was for me some of the tensest minutes I've ever experienced, he returned with an all clear. Moments after crossing into the U.S., I pulled off the road into a quiet spot, leaned back on my seat, and just gave thanks to God—again and again. Once in the U.S., I contacted U.S. Customs and Border Control, and learned there was a facility at the Dulles Airport in Virginia (about an hour away) that was set up to deal with situations such as mine, thus obviating the need to return all the way back to Canada.

God is so good!

I commenced my work at the *Adventist Review* office on October 17, 1988, in the old Review and Herald building, located in the section of the old GC complex that lay within the District of Columbia. Other buildings in the complex, literally across the street, were in in Takoma Park, in the State of Maryland. The GC's location grew on me in a big hurry, and (with many others) I lamented the move to the office's present location in Silver Spring (Maryland), even though it was to more spacious surroundings.

With all the trauma of moving from Canada, I expected to be given ample time (about three weeks, at least) to get my bearings and come up to speed. Instead, Editor-in-chief Bill Johnsson informed me with a straight face that I was down for an editorial, due in four days!

And thus it was, unexpectedly, that I hit the ground running. And running was, indeed, the operable word throughout my time at the magazine. Putting out a weekly journal is not a task for slouches. The deadlines keep coming good and plenty, often reminding me of that scene in *I Love Lucy*, featuring Lucy and Ethel in a chocolate factory, trying to wrap candy pieces coming at them fast and furious on an unrelenting conveyor belt.

Only it wasn't chocolate for me.

But it was pleasant work, nonetheless—pleasant in terms of the intangible rewards. The reward, in particular, of having the privilege of speaking to tens of thousands of fellow Adventists (and others) on a monthly basis—sometimes even more frequently. And the reward of meeting and mingling with God's people in their churches and gatherings literally all around the world.

There were rough times, of course. For while the overwhelming response from readers to what I wrote was positive—sometimes even glowing—not too infrequently there were other readers who begged to differ, even strongly. Once, in response to something I'd written, one Adventist gentleman, instead of writing, sent a tape to the office, with a voice so chilling I got the impression that if he would have run into me in a dark place, he could actually have inflicted bodily harm.

That's how tough it can get writing for the general Adventist public. We have some interesting saints out there. But I'd bought into the idea, ever since I heard it at one of the annual professional writers' conventions we attended, that an editorial is not a devotional. Rather, it's an opinion on some current issue facing the church (or facing society, with implications for the church.) This meant that my editorials dealt with real issues, affecting (and sometimes involving) real contemporary people, churches, or institutions. And that approach could sometimes touch people's nerves.

Looking back, I'm amazed at the volume of material created in this way. When Stanborough Press in the U.K. invited me to bring together a selection of my editorials for a book, I was genuinely surprised to see how many editorials I'd written over the years—and surprised too by their variety. [See the selection in Roy Adams, *From the Heart: Issues Facing the Church, Society—and You* (Alma Park, Grantham, Lincs.: Stanborough Press Ltd., 2007.)]

Apart from editorials, loads of articles came from my pen over the years. They connected me to Adventist believers around the world in ways I could not have anticipated. When I would arrive for appointments, even in far-away places, I was running into a multitude of people who felt they already knew me and what I stood for. Scary sometimes, but most times very gratifying.

It was a privilege I wouldn't have exchanged for anything. And I want to expand on this in the chapter that follows.

CHAPTER 12

Best of Times: My Tenure at the *Adventist Review*

THROUGHOUT THE YEARS of Bill Johnsson's term as editor in chief of *Adventist Review* (which was the bulk of my time there), the spirit at the office was superb. There was a sense of working together for a common goal, a common product; and each week we got to see the result of our labor in print. It was an exhausting assignment, involving a multitude of details and unending deadlines. But one felt good about going to work in the morning. It was a pleasant, creative place to be.

And this was due in no small measure to the one in charge, Dr. William G. Johnsson. Johnsson had his moments, of course, as do we all, I suppose—a handful of days when he would seem uncharacteristically testy, and for no apparent reason. Together with others on the staff, I've been at the short end of that testiness on more than one occasion, leaving me wondering each time: *What was that about? And what did I do to provoke or deserve it?*

But those were the exceptions—count them on the fingers on one hand, if you will. The norm was that Johnsson was one of the most decent leaders one can ever hope to work with, hands down. He had his feet on the ground; was sure of his own identity; and was big enough to give editors the slack they each needed to operate as responsible adults. He was calm in those embarrassing moments when something controversial appeared in print, sending some of the saints into apoplexy, and making us the depository of harsh letters, emails, and phone calls. Even when it was something that left us all embarrassed—as when the wrong telephone number appeared in the magazine, a number for a certain "adult" service. Somehow he knew we could ride it out—and we did. And, so far as I can recall, he didn't come down on the person or persons that might have been responsible for the blunder.

Under Johnsson, editors felt free to operate, free to move, free to be creative. He did not micromanage. In his time we looked for any excuse to have a party—a birthday, the arrival of a new staff member (temporary or not), the departure of an intern, whatever. We'd gather in our little library (which doubled as a conference room) to celebrate. And Christmastime would often find us gathered in his home, hosted by his wife Noelene, singing carols, listening to Christmas stories, and—of course—generously feeding our faces. All this in addition to our annual retreats when, leaving the work of the office behind, we'd go to some quiet spot for Friday night and Sabbath, ending with a social Saturday evening. If such a social happened to include a story by Johnsson, then we all waited in anticipation. He is a master story-teller!

Bill and I happened to be of the same political leaning, and often he'd drop by my office, shut the door behind him, and sit down for a little powwow on the events of the day. For many years, our two families would eat Thanksgiving dinner together—at their place or ours. Bill is a New Testament scholar of no mean caliber, and it was always a joy to sit at his feet when he was in charge of the devotional for our weekly staff meetings. He would speak about New Testament characters as if he knew them personally, and about New Testament events as if he'd been present as an eyewitness.

The point is that he made the *Review* office a very pleasant place to work.

Looking beyond the confines of our office in Silver Spring,

Maryland, I think that one of the extraordinary privileges I enjoyed while working at the General Conference (GC) for the *Review* was the opportunity to meet fellow Adventists all around the world in their various countries and localities. Few things gave me greater joy. To come face to face with them; to see how they worship, how they witness, how they live their faith; to get a small taste of the realities they confront each day. And then to return to the office and, in a series of (what we then called) Editor's Reports, share the experience with the global Adventist family.

In many respects, this period and this activity constituted the best time of my entire ministry. A few random vignettes of these travels come to mind.

Poland

In Poland for a youth retreat in the summer of 1991, I was housed in a large dormitory-style building just outside the main tent. From my room, when I was not myself speaking, I could hear the various other meetings in progress (though they were all in Polish, except when the visiting Australian singing group, New Testament, was up front). And what impressed me over the period of my stay was the hunger of these young people for the word of God. I spoke twice a day—morning and evening. But between those times, the program continued, stopping only at mealtime—though even then, there would usually be some practice or rehearsal taking place.

Such overseas visits sometimes called for quick and unexpected adjustments to the situation on the ground. I remember looking under the bathroom curtain and seeing the feet of someone who seemed to be taking an eternity in the shower one morning, a time when I needed a quick wet-down following my morning walk, and before breakfast. Since my room was just across the hallway from the facility, I made two or three trips to check on the progress of this fastidious bather. Imagine my surprise when a woman emerged from the place! Only then did I realize that both male and female were using the same toilet and shower facilities. After that, I simply rolled with the punches.

Like anyone traveling for the church, I learned to expect the unexpected—in regard, for example, to being roped in for talks and presentations not on the agreed schedule. But however much I'd learned to expect such things, I was still taken by surprise every now and again. And it happened in Poland.

"We are going down to the town today," my host said to me one morning, "and we want you to go with us."

Well, sure, I could make time for that. Will give me a chance to see another Polish town—just about 20 minutes away from the lakeside campground where we were meeting. But as we're driving to the place, I say to him, out of curiosity: "So what are we going to do in the town?"

His response surprised me. In the most beautiful Polish English, he said: "You will be speaking there."

I chuckled inside to think that I came by that intelligence at that point only because of my own curiosity. Left to him, the information would have come even later. I remember that as I began my impromptu speech in front of the constantly changing crowd that had gathered in the square within earshot of the Catholic Church compound, the first words to stumble out of my lips were: "I bring you greetings from the people of the United States and from the president of the United States, where I live just about 12 miles, as the crow flies, from the White House."

I have no idea how all that came across in translation, but I could see mouths fall open as the people realized that they were standing in the presence of someone who lives just 12 miles away from the most powerful house on earth! And what they probably didn't realize is that those 12 miles may as well be twelve hundred miles, for all the access they give me to the president. But how else could I make small talk before launching into a totally unexpected spiritual presentation in front of a motley crowd of total strangers?

Later that day, I was taken to visit the mayor of another nearby town, and I remember facing a simple but most difficult question from the gentleman moments after we sat down. Learning who I was and what I was doing, his question was direct: "With Poland almost one hundred per cent Christian, why did you come?"

Try answering that question from the lips of a Roman Catholic town mayor in the heart of a Roman Catholic country. That's when you take a page from some of the annoying politicians around Washington, who could never give a straightforward answer to the most direct of questions. Whatever I said, and however it came across in translation, the mayor seemed pleased, and gave me the key to the town.

Following our meetings, my hosts took me to several places of interest around Poland, including the world-famous city of Gdańsk, whose shipyards on the Baltic Sea became the birthplace of Poland's Solidarity Movement, an uprising that eventually brought down the communist governments not only of Poland, but also of other countries throughout the entire former Soviet Bloc.

It was a good visit. And my most indelible memory was the dedication and commitment of the young people, and their hunger for the things of the Spirit.

Inter-American Division

In July of 1993, I travelled in the Inter-American Division with communication director Leslie McMillan, making stops in Venezuela, Colombia, Panama, Guyana, Curacao, and Haiti—gathering materials for a series of editor's reports in the *Review*. Arriving in Colombia on a Sunday morning, I remember being taken into the well-protected offices of the local conference there in Bogota, the nation's capital, for a meeting with conference leaders. As we sat down, I was visibly startled by explosions outside, not far away. "Firecrackers," they quickly explained to this rattled visitor. "It's fiesta time, and people are celebrating." With that explanation, I relaxed and settled in for our meeting.

But the fiesta, notwithstanding, things were still tense in the country. And when we arrived in Medellin, the local leaders would not allow us to stay at any hotel in the city, out of concern for our safety. Instead, they put us up in a guest house on the large, fenced-in campus, home to both the North Colombia Union and Colombia Adventist University. But whether on the campus or traveling around Medellin, there was no time when I experienced any real fear, such as I did that first Sunday at the conference office in Bogota.

In conversations with university personnel, we were regaled with hair-raising stories of opposition and persecution by the dominant (Roman Catholic) church in the 1950s and 60s—opposition that forced members at one point, for example, to dig an underground tunnel to their secret meeting place. They told how, in one instance, a plan had been laid to poison the water supply of the budding educational institution that eventually blossomed into the present university; and how God miraculously intervened to scuttle the nefarious scheme. The man designated to pull off the wicked act went into town to purchase the poison and, before returning home, drank himself drunk to numb his conscience for the evil deed. However, thinking he would need even more spirits before the actual job, he brought a bottle home with him. And in his drunken state (his wife, who later became Adventist, told them), he drank from the wrong bottle, and the toxic mix that was supposed to poison the campus's water supply killed him instead.

As we arrived at our hotel on the outskirts of Caracas (Venezuela), on a Friday afternoon, I took note of the picturesque hills that overlooked the place. I must get up there, I said to myself. But with a sermon plus another assignment to prepare for the next day, I knew the trip to the hills would have to wait. Yet lingering in my mind was the terrific view one could get from there.

So after working on my sermon and other things Friday evening, I woke early Sabbath for a morning walk to those very hills, looking forward to the panoramic scene from the place as the sun rose. I left the hotel about six-o'clock, my camera hanging from my shoulder and my wallet in my pocket—thinking it would be safer with me than in my hotel room! Zigzagging my way through the nearby residential area, my nose was pointed in the general direction of the hills.

It was on one of those residential streets, fortunately not far from the hotel, that a car just about grazed me as it flew by. That surprised me, given the wideness of the road and the fact that there was no other traffic that early in the morning. But I thought little more of it, and kept going, hoping to find some short-cut that would lead me to my destination. But when the same vehicle came back down the road, this time driving slowly, with its three male occupants ominously sizing me up, I smelled danger.

Acting on a whim that probably came from a divine source, I pushed my right hand down my pocket and came up with what I hoped would look to them like a piece of paper, and acted as if I were verifying an address. Perhaps momentarily confused, they drove by without stopping. Which gave me enough time to bolt into a side street, and beat a hasty retreat to the hotel.

Over lunch after my sermon that day, I mentioned the incident in conversation. "Where were you headed?" a brother asked, to make sure he'd heard me right. When I said it again, he and others around the table could hardly hide their disbelief. "That's one of the barrios," they said. "Even the police don't go there!"

Yet that's exactly where I was headed that morning!

In retrospect, I thank God for sending those thugs at that early morning hour to intercept my plans—plans that He knew had been conceived in complete innocence, not to say utter ignorance.

But the joy of the visit came from meeting our people; sitting down with them around the lunch table in their church, located in tight quarters amid prime real estate; hearing their questions and sharing their burdens during an afternoon open forum.

In **Haiti,** after visiting our hospital, our university, and the Adventist Development and Relief Agency (ADRA) facilities, we took in the evening evangelistic meetings then in progress in Port au Prince. I was blown away by the fervor we witnessed. In a single evening we visited three meeting sites, each one packed to the rafters! I was flabbergasted.

South America

In April, 1994, I travelled with Pastor Joao Wolff, then president of the South American Division, throughout his territory. We visited **Brazil** (taking in cities like Belem, Brasilia, Rio de Janeiro, Sao Paulo, Curitiba, and Porto Alegre); we visited **Chile** (with stops in Santiago and nearby towns); we stopped in **Peru** (taking in Lima, Cuzco, and Juliaca with its famous Lake Titicaca); **Ecuador** (stopping in Quito and Guayaquil); and we made a quick foray into La Paz, **Bolivia**.

In Belem I was impressed by the dedication of our medical workers, with our doctors and nurses engaged in active evangelism and other outreach ministry for the community. I remember being fascinated by our media ministry in Rio; intimidated by the immense size of Sao Paulo; and captivated by the multi-cultural ministry being carried on in Santiago, where an evening meeting featured (among others) police officers, Jews, Arabs, and Gypsies. It was gratifying to hear their testimonies about what the Adventist message was beginning to mean for them.

Riding in a boat on Lake Titicaca one damp afternoon, I mentally tried to retrace the steps of Fernando and Ana Stahl. I tried to imagine the loneliness and privations they must have encountered in the early days of our work in the region, with no local church infrastructure for support, such as I was enjoying during my visit.

My reports on that South American trip ran through four major articles in the magazine (in August of 1994); and all I can share in the space available here is nostalgia. I left the area with a single, overriding impression of our people in the region: They're consumed with fire—holy fire for the gospel.

Central and Southern Africa-Indian Ocean Region

Several trips to the central and southern Africa region took me to places like Cote D'Ivoire, Ghana, Kenya, Zimbabwe, Botswana, and South Africa. Each one with stories of their own. In one trip to South Africa, for example, I covered the conversations then taking place between segregated entities of our church, with the goal of unity.

Clearly I cannot even begin to describe here how much I learned.

But it's my visit to **Madagascar** sometime in 1994 that stands out in my head at this moment of writing. The picture of that Sabbath morning crowd—the specter of some 7,000 Adventists in that huge, open-air amphitheater in Antananarivo, listening to the word of God—made an unforgettable impression in my mind. And to watch hundreds of them come forward during the appeal was sheer joy.

Yet I'm remembering the tragic death in a vehicular accident (a few years after my visit) of the person who was union president of that field when I went through there; and the more recent death of the wife of the person who served as my translator during the visit, and who later became president the Southern Africa-Indian Ocean division, of which Madagascar is a part. It serves as a stark reminder that we have no abiding city here; that we're only pilgrims passing through.

Numerous other trips took me to **England, the Caribbean, Australia, and elsewhere**—for camp meetings, retreats, seminars, conference and union constituency sessions. Perhaps Australia was my most frequent stop, and I cannot even now remember the number of appointments I took there. The journey was long, and they worked you to the bones, but I had a love affair going with the place and people, and found myself saying yes to their invitation almost every time. It was in Australia that I encountered for the first time that world famous food spread known as Marmite. My first taste of the yeast-derived product repelled me, largely because, in my ignorance, I'd spread the stuff too thick. After that, under the most gentle and gracious prodding of my hosts at each visit, I would sample the product, ever so gingerly. Until, eventually, I grew to like it—indeed, to enjoy it, finding myself looking forward to breakfast (especially), so I could spread it on my bread, topped with avocado and jam and peanut butter.

I did other travel appointments for the church, both before and after joining the GC and the *Adventist Review*—too numerous to describe in detail. I'm remembering the trip to the U.K. in August 1997, which coincided with the tragic death of Princess Diana on a subway street in Paris; the trip to Malaysia when, flying into the country, I read the ominous notice on the landing card that *"the penalty for drug possession in Malaysia is death"*—a warning that gives one the tremors, however clean they think they are, wondering whether anything they might be carrying could be construed as a violation); my trip to Mission College for their graduation, and the big surprise of finding an Adventist college campus of such spectacular beauty in the heart of Thailand's countryside. (Incidentally, one unexpected bonus of that Mission College trip was the visit by a member of the country's Royal Family to deliver the commencement address, a visit that brought with it a large measure of security, suspense, and drama.)

Rubbing Shoulders with Non-Adventists

My global appointments also included non-Adventist meetings and convocation, among them two World Council of Churches (WCC) general assemblies—the first in the Australian capital of **Canberra** and the second in **Harare**, Zimbabwe's capital.

One incident from Canberra comes to mind.

It was February 1991, the height of the Australian summer, when the Canberra assembly convened. And the oppressive heat was to provide an opportunity for a few over-zealous Adventists to put the name of the church in awful bad light in front of the international body.

Three Adventist church leaders attended the Canberra meetings: Longtime Adventist religious liberty champion Dr. Bert Beach was there as an observer, an official designation for important non-member attendees. Together with others in his category, he was seated on the ground floor, at the back of the hall, right behind the delegates. Raymond Coombe, public affairs and religious liberty director for the South Pacific Division (headquartered in Sydney, Australia) was there to report for his division. And I was attending with press credentials from the *Adventist Review.* Both Ray and I (with the rest of the international press corps), sat on a side balcony overlooking the assembly.

Over the course of the first two days, all three of us had been accosted, more than once, by one or another of four feisty, opinionated Adventists belonging to a group some Australian Adventists derisively call "the concerned brethren." At least a couple of them at a time would post themselves near the entrance of the meeting place each day, handing out tracks to delegates going in and out—or to whomever would receive them. In the role of reporter, I considered it part of my duty to talk and listen to them, and try to understand their point of view, however zany. Security was tight, and these guys (like other demonstrators and curiosity seekers) were not allowed inside the auditorium.

But sometime around the third day of the session, the building's air-conditioning system broke down; and by mid-afternoon, as the heat inside the hall reached unbearable levels, the side doors into the main (ground) floor were ordered open.

As if anticipating precisely that development (I've still not stopped marveling at their uncanny timing), three of these four Adventist protesters marched into the hall, and in full view of the assembly's 3000 (astonished) delegates, hoisted a banner attached to helium balloons high up into the ceiling, reading: "Seventh-Day Adventists Believe... This Prophecied Romeward Unity Is the Spirit of Anti-Christ!"

Instantly, Bert, Ray, and I knew we had a crisis on our hands. Three disgruntled Adventists had taken it upon themselves to besmirch the church's good name in front of the whole world. Regardless of what the Adventist Church believes, no thinking Adventist would disrupt someone else's meeting to make their point. Fundamental decorum and courtesy would dictate otherwise.

As the entire session grounded to a halt, and the minds of council officials went into overdrive as to how to take the offending banner down (eventually, they'd have to bring in a cherry picker to do the job), Bert, Ray, and I made eye contact and quickly left the hall for a hasty confab outside, under the watchful eye, as we later learned, of at least one of the four Adventist brothers who'd executed the mischievous scheme. (In a document from them that came to my hand in the days following, I read a description of exactly what Bert, Ray, and I did—separately and together—following the incident. We had no idea where the three went after hoisting the banner and leaving the hall, but probably the fourth man had us under constant surveillance.)

Bert Beach, we decided in our quick huddle, would take the extraordinary step of asking permission to make a statement before the assembly, a near unprecedented occurrence for an attendee in his category. Permission was granted, and Bert did us proud, setting the church's record straight in his own eloquent, inimitable style. The assembly was satisfied—and consoled.

But I perceived that the potential for damage was not quite over with Bert's apology. The moment the banner went up, dozens of cameras clicked to immortalize the image. I couldn't control that. But I knew that, like me, many reporters, in spite of having cameras of their own, depended on the official photos provided by the Council itself. Daily numbered copies of available shots were posted on a large bulletin board outside the upstairs balcony. Reporters would then order the images they wanted by number.

I arrived early the following day to look for the image of the offending banner, and there it was. If that (numbered) item is removed from the board, it likely would not be missed, the commotion of the previous day notwithstanding. Standing there, I knew what I had to do—for me a very strange and unusual act (not unlike God's own unusual action described in Isaiah 28:21, as I conveniently reasoned). Asking God for a special indulgence, I took the damaging image down and "filed" it away.

That whole banner episode aside, the WCC assembly events were a good experience—both in Canberra and Harare. Rubbing shoulders for some eight days with Christians of other communions and people of other faiths from around the world is both inspiring and educational. One comes away with a realization of how much we Adventists can learn from others, with a sense of the complexity of our own mission, and with a better understanding of our special place in the vast scheme of things.

Other Things that Brought Me Joy

It was not just experiences with Adventists around the world that made my tenure with the *Adventist Review* the best of times. It was also the privilege I had of communicating with Adventists on the ground in North America, where most of our readers live. Through their letters to the editor, their letters to me personally, their telephone calls, and my interaction with them as I travelled across the division, I received a lift, a buoyancy, that I find difficult to put into words. It was almost as if they and I had something personal going between us, and as if there weren't other editors in the mix.

To be sure, I received my share of brickbats—it went with the territory. And although my intention was never to offended readers, I always knew I could never please everyone. Even Jesus in his ministry did not achieve that result—in fact, He fell far short of it. But in all my writings I tried to be kind, even when handling sensitive and difficult issues.

The affirmation I received, from time to time—not from "the brethren," but from the grassroots—was overwhelming. And here I pick out at random just one example of such intimate encouragement and support, an example I stumbled on quite by accident while leafing through a few back copies of the *Adventist Review* in preparation for this memoir.

It came in the form of a greeting card and accompanying letter, arriving on my desk January 25, 2006, from Richard Selzer, office manager of the Redding Seventh-day Adventist Church in California. When he became office manager, his idea was to send out a card or two every week to the church's shut-ins. But in time the idea broadened to include several other categories of members; and then, eventually (and that's where I came in) it came to include some person or some organization from the division featured in that quarter's mission emphasis.

I was so impressed by that gesture from the Redding Church that I wrote a Thanksgiving editorial about it, dated November 23, 2006. And here's how the editorial described the touching beauty of what that church was doing (although I cannot now remember how I happened to come across the editorial's opening illustration that appears in the first lines below):

"One of those who received the [Redding] *church's thank-you card was Judy Heinrich, for many years a coworker with her husband Oscar in the production of 'Mission Spotlight,' shown in Sabbath schools around the world. The Redding church's letter came at a special moment for her, she said in a letter to them. 'When I arrived at the office this morning,' she wrote, 'it was almost more than I could handle because it was just three years ago tonight that my husband, Oscar, had a heart attack and passed away.' Just before the church's letter arrived that afternoon, one of her daughters had brought to her office a bouquet of flowers in memory of her dad. 'I was sitting at my desk trying to absorb their beauty,' Mrs. Heinrich wrote, 'when she came back in, placed your letter and card in my hands, and said, "I cannot believe this came right at this time!"'"*

"The church's thoughtful gesture," *I wrote,* "had arrived just in time to lift the spirits of a bereaved spouse bravely struggling to carry on."

Our situations are all different. I was not grieving like Mrs. Hendricks that January day as the Redding church's card arrived on my desk. But as I wrote in the editorial, "there's probably not a single one of us who does not appreciate a word of encouragement from time to time. And truth be told, mine is a lonely—and sometimes thankless—job." "But that cold winter day... the letter from the Redding church arrived to brighten the drabness."

And here's what Brother Selzer wrote in the card accompanying the letter: "We are sending you a card just to say thank you. Thank you for your years of service to our church, for your wisdom and insight, and for the thoughtful and intelligent way you present that wisdom and insight. We pray God's continued blessings and leading in your life." And the card was signed by more than 30 of the members, none of whom (including Selzer) had ever met me personally.

"How precious!" my editorial continued. *"Apart from the*

heavenly agencies themselves, these are the people who give me the inspiration to go on—inspiration to write one more article, attend one more committee, preach one more sermon, work one more day. Often nameless, these are the people I live for. And what I like about [the Redding church's] expression of gratitude is that it came with no strings attached, no hook at the end, no product to sell. 'We send cards for no special reason except to say thank you.'"

Many neat things happened to me during my time at the *Review*, but that was one of the most touching. It was the best of times—my tenure at the magazine.

Part II

)))

He will not judge by what he sees with his eyes,
or decide by what he hears with his ears;
but with righteousness he will judge the needy,
with justice he will give decisions for the poor of the earth.
.... Righteousness will be his belt
and faithfulness the sash around his waist.
Isaiah 11:3-5

But let justice roll down like waters,
and righteousness like an ever-flowing stream.
Amos 5:24, NRSV

Political systems come and go. Societal values keep changing.
Selfishness, racial prejudice, pride, abuse, envy, and greed will simply find a new, more politically correct form of expression as social
climates change.

Chantal and Gerald Klingbeil,
Adventist World, Nov 2011, p. 19

It is tact that is golden, not silence.
Samuel Butler

Heading into Troubled Waters

MY NATURAL INCLINATION and preference—especially at this point in my life—would be to write "nice" things, pleasing things, things that would engender warm, cozy feelings and hearty Amens.

Unfortunately, however, my experience has led me to see a little of the Adventist Church's under-belly, and my story would be incomplete—even dishonest and misleading—if I failed to go there, enough at any rate to create a more comprehensive picture. What I find is that with the passage of time, the reality and implications of the events I relate in the next five chapters begin to recede in memory—more and more seeming to have never taken place. And I got to thinking that if that's the case with me *to whom they actually happened,* how much more so for those who only witnessed them from a distance.

Hence the growing conviction I experienced to share those chapters of my journey, however painful.

The conviction was so strong, in fact, that I felt I had to write it all down, even without any assurance they'd ever see the light of day. At least, I thought, my own children deserve to know (since at the moment they have only a vague idea); my wife deserves to know (for though she witnessed many of the events described, she could not enter my inner thoughts and feelings); and my relatives and close friends would want to know (for obvious reasons).

In addition, I was convinced that there were loads of people all around me during the time these things were happening—as well as

Review readers across North America and beyond—who hadn't the foggiest idea what actually went down. I think they too deserve to know. To know how "the brethren" function; to know what sometimes goes on in the smokeless cloakrooms of Adventist officialdom; and how desperately people can vie for position and power "within the fold." My experience provides, I think, a case in point that can be instructive for those who come after—especially those who look like me.

I wish I could remember more, but my journaling efforts have been sporadic, at best. At the end of the typical day I find myself utterly spent; and keeping a written record of that day's happenings was usually the very last thing on my mind. Nevertheless, I did make the occasional journal entries, especially at critical times of my life; and these chapters will rely heavily on those entries. In fact, at many points, I will quote verbatim from those notes, particularly when I want to allow the reader to enter into my feelings and mood at critical times in the story.

(For easy recognition, materials lifted from my journal appear in italics, framed by quotation marks at the beginning and at the end—not in front of every paragraph, as is the usual custom for citations. Quotation marks for statements attributed to others are used only when I can remember what they said fairly accurately, having written them down very soon after the encounters in question.)

Once I made the decision to share these experiences, I had to decide what to include and what to leave out—for though my journal entries were only occasional, I was surprised by their sheer volume. If at any time you think I'm saying too much, then you should see what I've left out! And if at any time you wonder if things really got that bad, then my answer is that I'm not even telling all. But I'm sharing sufficient, I hope, to give a rounded picture, leaving out anything I thought might come across as trite, mean-spirited, or unkind.

I'm into uncharted territory here, having found no models in the church for what I'm doing. In the church, we sanitize things. We tweak the minutes of meetings, for example, to reflect a positive tone, to give the impression that everything was hunky-dory. It makes us feel better. And being not immune to this general mindset, I struggled with how to tell my story. For as with any story, other characters are involved apart from me—characters that come with names attached. No problem when the tale is rosy—people like to get an honorable mention then, sometimes even taking umbrage if not included. But when the saga takes a negative turn, that's when folk would rather have their names left out.

With that in mind, I grappled with the issue of how to proceed, at one point even toying with the idea of presenting chapters 13 to 17 in the form of parable, using fictitious names; or in the form of allegory—a la George Orwell's *Animal Farm*. But in the end I thought either approach seemed a tad too cute. Apart from the inherent difficulty of that style of writing, I couldn't presume that readers would have either the time or the inclination to try to decipher the complicated nuances of my story through parables or riddles.

So finally, I decided to go for the straightforward approach and tell the story as it happened, names and all. Only to take care to be so accurate that no one named could possibly deny the truthfulness of what I report. The fact of the matter is that other people did become part of my overall story and, where appropriate for painting the full picture, they deserve a mention—whether negative or positive. The names that will feature most frequently would be that of former GC president, Jan Paulsen; former *Adventist Review/Adventist World* editor, William G. Johnsson; and former *AR/AW* associate editor (and, as I write, editor in chief), Bill Knott. (Because of long standing familiarity, I will frequently refer to Johnsson and Knott as Bill J and Bill K, respectively—and to Knott as simply "Bill," wherever the context makes it clear that Bill Johnsson had departed the scene). Other names will be identified as they appear.

Throwing stones is not my purpose here, living as I do in a house of glass myself. I simply want to tell my story faithfully. And in that regard, I'm not myself untouchable. For however painful—and as the account warrants—I will mention some of my own foibles, misjudgments, weaknesses, vulnerabilities, fears, and embarrassments. But whether dealing with myself or with others, my intent would never be to let it all hang out. That would serve no good purpose. Without deliberately omitting any exculpatory evidence that I know, I seek to provide just enough information to set the scene and make the case.

So in the end, I found myself unable to keep silent. To quote a line from Samuel Butler, "It is tact that is golden, not silence." For what it's worth, I think I owe it to posterity to tell what happened—with courage, prudence, and tact; holding myself to the highest standards of accuracy, integrity, and fairness.

CHAPTER 13

A Peace Disturbed—Editor Changing, Tensions Rising

AT A FORMAL retirement function for me, staged by the *Adventist Review* office in the atrium of the General Conference (GC) complex toward the end of 2010, both Bill Knott and (new) GC President Ted Wilson made comments to the effect that "Roy is the longest serving associate editor in the history of the *Adventist Review*." A retirement program is somewhat like a preview of one's funeral; you get to hear some of the nice things folks have to say about you, now that you're off the stage and practically powerless—as if in death. Both men meant their remarks as a compliment, of course. But what they saw as something to be lauded, I saw as the very epitome of *dead-end*.

And that, in part, is the story of chapters 13-17.

The long, drawn-out events surrounding the replacement of the *Adventist Review* editor began (for me) at a long-range planning day away from the office, September 14, 2005. In the midst of a lengthy, (uncharacteristically) rambling worship talk to begin the day, Bill Johnsson announced to the staff that that was going to be his last (annual) planning session with us. He then went into considerable detail regarding his conversation with then GC president Jan Paulsen and the commitment he'd made to him to (among other things) hold on a little longer to see the new magazine, *Adventist World,* on its feet.

(Incidentally, earlier that year, Paulsen had called me to his office to inform me that Bill Johnsson had expressed his determination to hang it up, and that Paulsen and his committee had extended an invitation to Dr. John McVay, then dean of Andrews University Theological Seminary, to join the *Review* as editor in chief. As a courtesy, he wanted to give me a heads-up. In the end, McVay, one of the most decent Adventist church leaders I know—and whom I'd have been delighted to work "under"—turned down the call; which threw the Administration back to square one.)

Bill J's remarks at that planning meeting created an uncomfortable time for me. I remember fellow editor Bonita Shields (sitting next to me during our prayer request time) innocently asking me to offer special prayer after the two staff members who'd already been assigned—special prayer for God's guidance over the choice of a successor. I demurred, telling her later that, given the circumstances, I did not consider such a public prayer on my part appropriate. The following week at staff meeting, after I'd already been tagged to pray, fellow editor Steve Chavez openly (and again innocently) requested that I include that detail among the prayer items. In that case, I did, keeping it as brief as possible. Clearly, because I was completely mum on the matter, other editors did not understand how sensitive the issue was for me.

On October 5, 2005, with annual council set to begin in two days, Bill J in staff meeting again brought up the matter of his replacement. "I think they're talking about it," he said, "although I have no idea what exactly they have in mind or if they will have the nominating committee bring in a name next week."

It was a nervous time for me. Not because I sought the job. In fact, as people throughout my travels would broach the subject (to my keen embarrassment), I'd told the Lord again and again that I really would prefer not to have the job—although I was prepared to make a go of it, if that was His will. My reticence came not from a lack of ambition, but from having looked up-close at the load Bill J carried. It was heavy—and complex. I felt I had little stomach for many of the inevitable political intrigues associated with the job. And for reasons known only to me, I also felt unworthy of the responsibility.

As it turned out, the item never surfaced at the 2005 Annual Council.

But my attempts to shift the subject to the back of my head did not prevent others from continuing to bring it forward. One such occasion happened in early December (2005), when former GC Public Relations and Religious Liberty director Bert Beach dropped by my office for a chat, bringing up the matter of Bill J's succession, as umpteen others had done. *"I should by now know what to say,"* I wrote in my journal later, *"but somehow I still don't. The matter is so awkward and sensitive. I usually end up saying I have no idea what will happen; that it's not a given that one of the two associates would be picked; that Bill J intends to stay on for a while to see* Adventist World *up and running; and that anyone who, knowing the complexity of Bill's job as I do, sits on the edge of their seat waiting for it, is crazy."*

"It's not easy to make a decision between you [and Bill K]," Beach said to me. "I mean, you are two competent guys! And to put one above the other is not easy. Usually in such cases they bring in someone from the outside who doesn't have a clue, and whom you both have to bring up to speed."

Needless to say, this was awkward talk for me, and my unspoken reaction came on many levels. One of them was the frustration of being always evaluated in tandem—"Both of you are equally... [whatever]," On another level it tended to create the impression that I was myself running competition or vying for the office. For someone like me, who has spent their whole career lamenting the craving for power and control in the church, such comparisons had become obnoxious and wearying. Only the Lord knew how much I wanted out of that situation. I envied people who got calls to this position or that; and was prepared to leave my current job in a heartbeat, if something suitable would have opened up—something that did not involve a move from the area (which would have disrupted my wife's career); and something that was consistent with my goals, aspirations, and competence. I wanted out of the perpetual rat-race at the *Adventist Review*—a pace that seemed to suck up time for adequate reading and reflection.

The situation vis-à-vis the editor's position, deferred during the 2005 Annual Council, would come up at the 2006 Spring Meeting, scheduled for April 12 and 13 on the campus of Loma Linda University in California. And on Wednesday March 22, three weeks before those meetings opened, my world changed. That's the day my assistant, Larie Gray, brought a telephone message in to me as an editors' meeting on design was ending. It read: "Paulsen would like to see you. Now, if possible."

As I headed for his office that morning in no particular hurry, my mind quickly scoured the field, searching for a possible reason for the urgent summons. *It could be only one thing,* I thought. And when we sat down, he went right to it, (pasted) warm smile in place.

"Roy, you would recall that one year ago, we talked about the matter of succession at the *Adventist Review*. Well, recently, Bill [Johnsson] talked to me again." (He then went on to explain how this time Johnsson felt he should call it quits—because of his family situation, etc.) "And we have been grappling with his successor," he continued. (I'm still in suspense at this point). "You'd recall that last time we went outside the staff, but the person we looked at—things did not work out that way. [As indicated above, Dr. John McVay had declined the invitation.] The vice presidents and I comprise a sort of informal search committee, and we have looked at the matter again, and have decided to go with a member of the staff. We've decided to ask Bill Knott to serve." (I was not surprised, and I don't think the emotion on my face changed a single bit upon receiving the information).

"It was a tough decision [the usual cliché]. Both you men are talented and competent. For *Adventist Review* editor, we look for men who are balanced, who are neither leaning to the right or to the left, but who would operate from the center. And both you men meet that criterion." (Here he probably forgot—or chose not to remember—that a year earlier, he'd explained that one of the reasons they'd not turned to me was that I came across as somewhat controversial; that some things I'd written had ruffled feathers and stirred up passion in some sectors of the church. Now he was about to present a new reason why I'd not been chosen.) "Editors of the *Adventist Review* have historically served for extended periods," he said—mentioning as examples F.D. Nichol, Kenneth Wood, and, most recently, Bill Johnsson (who up to that time had been editor in chief for some 22 years); "and we want someone who can give that kind of extended service."

Translation: you're too old for the job.

When some unsuitable person logically stands in line to succeed an "important" retiring leader, a typical strategy for the powers that be in the Adventist Church is to ask the outgoing occupant of the position to stay on a little longer. In the case of *Adventist Review*, I estimate that Paulsen moved to delay Bill J's retirement for some three to four years. Which means (and here, like Paul, "I speak as a fool") that had Johnsson retired when he had first wanted to, I'd have been 61 or 62. And that would have given me (I indulge in this foolishness only to make a point) 13 or 14 years of service as editor in chief, if I would have remained in the position up to Paulsen's age at the time he left office at 75. But the delay in Johnsson's retirement gave me time to catch up—time to reach the point of being too old for the job. Convenient, isn't it?

(I found it interesting that Paulsen would tag me for age! The same person who'd accepted the GC presidency in 1999 at age 64, gained reelection in 2005 at age 70, and would let his name stand in nomination in 2010, at age 75! But in 2006, at age 65, I was somehow too old to become *AR* editor. Talk about walking into a lawsuit for age discrimination! His words were as clear as day. And though I knew I'd never take the matter further, it was frightening to see how easily such a high-placed leader could inadvertently—and ignorantly—put the church in legal peril.) He hoped I would understand, he said, that his decision meant no depreciation of me.

His spiel done, he waited for my reaction.

For some reason that morning, I was as calm and as composed

as I can ever remember myself to be under similar circumstances. I happened to be wearing one of my best office outfits that particular day, and if, as they say, clothing adds something, I found myself very poised.

Paulsen has a nice way of (generally) not speaking to visitors to his office from behind his desk. And so that morning we sat facing each other, with no desk between us. Throughout his remarks (which lasted, I would estimate, about three minutes or so), I sat with my ten crossed (as his was), and looked him steadily in the eyes without averting my gaze. As I walked to his office, I'd surmised the reason for the meeting, and as his statement continued, I'd formed the conclusion before he actually got to it that I wouldn't be hearing my name as his choice. And once he announced the decision of his group, I knew I had nothing to lose thereafter. So without any meanness whatsoever, I was prepared calmly to steer him down and try to analyze what he was saying to me.

Whether it was to lessen the blow or for whatever other reason, he was at pains to emphasize, as he neared the end of his speech, that the decision was not yet final by any means. "The matter still has to go to the division presidents—and, you know," he said, "anything can happen." (Yeh, right!—as if he'd let it!) But he stressed that he wanted the two Bills and me to keep the matter under wraps, though he had no illusions about how things manage to get out.

My response was that I'd always left such matters in the hands of God, and was prepared to accept the outcome as His will. I'm sure I said more, but for the life of me I can't remember what that was. I didn't speak long, however—not by any means. I purposely kept my words as few and as vague as possible—I mean, what does one say under those circumstances? Lodge a protest? Request a recount? I remember thanking him for the briefing before I left.

Earlier that morning, Larie—who also served as Bill K's assistant—had brought in a note to him during the previous committee; and I remember him stepping out with no explanation as to where he was headed. By the time he returned, the committee on design was over. Then, during the following committee, it was my turn to be called away. And, like Bill K, I had to return to the office after hearing about my own fate and carry on with business as usual.

When I ran into Bill K down the hall late morning, I whispered: "Bill, I understand—confidentially—that congratulations are in order!"

"Well," he responded, "I hope you and I can sit down together soon about that. I'm still trying to understand what this all means." (He was speaking as if he was unprepared for the development and had been surprised by it.)

Later in the day, Bill J called us both into his office to talk about what had transpired during the morning. He recounted his family situation—again. And said how this time he needed to call it quits. He'd always felt, he said, that the leaders should look within the staff to fill the vacancy when he left, and he was gratified they were doing that. Either of us would have been a good choice, he said, repeating the familiar line. Now that Bill K had been chosen, he wanted me to know about his strong confidence in me and his deep appreciation for the talent and wisdom I brought to the staff. Bill K joined in with similar sentiments; and his tone of voice was almost as if Paulsen was to be faulted for making such an inappropriate decision.

The actor element in the guy was in top form that afternoon; like an undertaker trying to look sad at a 50,000-dollar funeral. I mean, his whole demeanor reflected a sense of empathy mixed with a touch of anxiety, and an O-my-dear,-how-could-Paulsen-do-such-a-thing look on his face. I sat there watching this. And when Bill J expressed his wish that some creative title might be devised to recognize my status under the new regime, Bill K heartily agreed. They both thought it would be bordering on disrespect to bring in a new associate and have that person listed on equal terms with me on the mastheads of the magazines, with no recognition of my senior status.

They meant well. But with the cold acceptance with which I'd received Paulsen's announcement of the morning, I now listened to them, inwardly rejecting completely any attempt at tokenism. It would be utterly unacceptable to me to have some highfalutin title devised purely as a sop for my apparent disappointment. Every bone in my body rejects such tomfoolery, however well meant.

I thanked them both for their kind words; but suggested we all "sleep on it." I was not keen on any artificial designation, I told them. If associate editor is what I am, then that's what should be on the magazines' mastheads.

My meeting with Paulsen came the day after the GC Ministerial Association's (televised) annual preaching seminar, held that year at a local area church, about 10 miles from the GC office. I was one of the speakers, and Paulsen showed up to give the welcome. He left immediately following, but not before we'd run into each other near the make-up room. His smile was as warm and as friendly as ever, even though by that time the decision had been made. Am I ever glad that that meeting with him in his office came after, and not before, I'd spoken at that seminar!

"As I write this," I entered into my journal the following Friday morning, two days later, "it's as if something in me has died. Truth be known, the editor's office is not a position I craved. In fact, observing it as closely as I did, I often wondered how I could ever pull it off, if it were offered to me. I felt it was too complicated for me, that I was not equal to the task. (But that's how I've always felt when confronting any important new assignment—so the feeling wasn't new. And I was always confident that if I had to, God would help me rise to the challenge.) Still, the finality of the [recent] action is just now hitting me— yesterday and today. It's as if there's no longer any reason to get up and go to work at the Review any more. I was passed over, plain and simple. And I feel more than a touch of injustice in that. After all, I've been at the AR now for more than 17 years. Bill K joined us, as I recall, less than 9 years ago. A huge chunk of that time, he spent working on his PhD, with the bare minimum of work at the office. It was a period of hardship for the entire staff, and a time of near slavery for me, as I struggled to keep up with my usual work, while catching many duties *that would ordinarily have fallen to him. Now with a doctorate in his hand for less than six months, the job is handed to him."*

One looks back on all those years of hard labor, and one remembers not a single word of commendation "from the top." Of course, there was always the ringing note of *general* appreciation ("You guys are doing a fantastic job with the magazines!"), but there was nothing ever personal. When the personal did come the previous year in Paulsen's office, it was for me to hear that some of the things I'd been writing were divisive and controversial.

A few days later, I shared with my journal what I'd been thinking as I walked in the early morning hours that day:

"I get the impression that my time is done at the magazine—that it's time to move on. The only question now is: where to? But I really feel tired of scheduling committees, manuscript evaluation, editing, art conferences, and endless committees on trouble-shooting. Wherever else I go, there'd be challenges, of course, but I'm a little tired of the old stuff. And the recent developments have only exacerbated the problem for me."

Surprise at Loma Linda

The 2006 Spring Meeting of the GC committee convened at Loma Linda, April 12 and 13; and on the agenda was the election of a new editor in chief for *Adventist Review/Adventist World*. In the period preceding such gatherings, a multitude of other meetings take place, one of the most important being that between the GC officers and the presidents of the church's world divisions. Bill Johnsson was invited by Paulsen to the spring confab of the presidents—"for one item," he said to some of us shortly before he left the office. (As it became clear later, that "one item" was the matter of the Adventist Review editorship—which naturally led to some speculation as to Johnsson's role at the special meeting. It would be hard to imagine the president inviting him in to oppose his choice on such a sensitive issue.)

The following Tuesday, word came that Johnsson wanted to speak to the staff the next day during our weekly staff meeting; and he did.

With all the aura of a reporter with an on-site dispatch, or the presenter at an awards ceremony, Johnsson took his time, throwing out morsels on this and that before "opening the envelope"—the content of which both Bill K and I already knew. Having that knowledge, I was left to squirm uneasily in my chair, as Johnsson excitedly spoke about his relief from knowing that a successor had been chosen. With the suspense on our end constantly building, Johnsson (delaying the announcement still further) told us how he'd called Noelene to tell her that "Today is the first day of the rest of my life."

Finally…finally, he was ready to open the envelope, the moment the entire staff had been waiting for. The presidents, he said deliberately, had chosen Bill Knott as editor in chief. And in the palpable awkwardness of the moment, congratulations went from all of us to Bill.

All this was happening on the eve of my own departure for Loma Linda for a meeting between senior editors and key Korean Adventist leaders involved in the operation and distribution of *Adventist World*, one of two such meetings we held each year (one in Seoul and the other in the U.S.) I would participate in that conference, then stay on for the Spring Meeting. Bill K would also make the trip for the same purpose, and with the added expectation, of course, of being elected editor in chief. Though I considered the outcome a fait accompli, it still was a tense period for me in the lead up to the critical vote.

I arrived in the Loma Linda area late Thursday night, April 6, and checked into the Hilton Hotel in San Bernardino. The next day, two things occupied my attention—locating the place for our (*Adventist World*) meeting Monday, and working on my income tax returns (which, with the April 15 deadline fast approaching, was still unfinished).

Sabbath morning, April 8, Paulsen spoke at the Loma Linda University church, praising the diversity of the church, and emphasizing unity and the need to love and care for each other. My response was, simply, *Wow!* (And I leave the reader free to interpret the exclamation.)

At breakfast in the Loma Linda University cafeteria Tuesday morning, April 11, I ran into an official from the inner circle of the GC, who came up to me with apparent genuine concern, mentioning how often he'd wished he could talk to me, but couldn't. That evening he reached me at my hotel, and at the end of our conversation, I made this entry to my journal: *"He wanted me to know, on deep background, how disappointed he was at the outcome of events surrounding the editorship, and how the reason given by Paulsen did not appeal to him. He indicated that he'd told Paulsen that in the United States today there's no set time for retirement—that a person could go on as long as they have the strength to. And he wanted me to know that I had a near unanimous support from the division presidents, and that he'd told Paulsen that he felt Roy should know about that support—and that Paulsen is planning to talk to me about it when we return to Washington. [The official] indicated that the entire vice-presidential team had constituted the search committee; and that Paulsen did not present the item to the division presidents as if canvassing their input, suggestion, or vote. Rather, it was presented as a report of the search committee. I found it gratifying to receive this behind-the-scenes account of things. [The official] felt there wasn't a single division president who would have come in with a name other than mine."*

This revelation brought back to mind how Paulsen, seeking somehow to lighten the blow when he'd given me the decision of the search committee, was at pains to emphasize that the item still had to go to the division presidents, that things could turn out differently, and that the decision was not final until all the votes were in. I now knew that the picture he painted had been disingenuous, if not outright deceptive, considering that he probably never intended that the division presidents would actually have a real say in the matter.

At steering committee Wednesday morning just ahead of the opening of Spring Meeting, GC under treasurer, Juan Prestol stood up to the president when he mentioned the matter of my age. "That's illegal in the United States," Prestol is reported to have said. But, alas, he had no support. North American Division secretary Roscoe Howard (who ordinarily would have backed him up), had miscalculated the time of the steering committee and was not present.

The Black leaders attending Spring Meeting perceived a racial bias in the proposed action; and during the morning, (then) Columbia Union president Harold Lee and Roscoe Howard led out in a series of ad hoc, small-group strategy sessions. To be sure, they'd begun rather late for that kind of effort, but things built quickly, and by early afternoon they had gotten their act together. Howard was even on the phone with Black conference presidents around the country, feeling them out on a strong response, should it come to that. "If they can do that to us on this issue," one African American leader said, "then they'll think they can walk all over us."

These leaders were going to stick their necks out for me—that was for sure. But they didn't approach the meeting with much hope, believing that Paulsen already had everything locked up.

I was in attendance as Spring Meeting convened Wednesday morning, April 12. And sometime during the proceedings, I'd seen Paulsen walk over to Bill J and whisper something to him. A little while later, Bill J had come over to me to say that "the Review item" will be coming up first thing in the afternoon, and Paulsen would prefer that both Bill K and I should not be present. So after lunch I returned to the hotel, prayed, took a short rest, and then got up to work on a Reflections piece for the *Review* that was coming due that week.

Turning momentarily to my journal, I made this entry: *"Right now, I'm in a daze. Sometimes it's as if it's not all happening to me. Some moments I feel I'm softening—as if I'd go on working at my present post; other moments I'm sure I need a change. My prayer goes out to you, Jesus, at this critical time of my life. However bad and embarrassing things look, I can still see your unfailing mercy and kindness."*

At about 5:30 p.m. (Pacific Time), as I worked on the Reflections piece, my telephone rang. It was Bill J. "Did you hear about the developments this afternoon?" he asked.

I didn't. So he proceeded to fill me in. And combining what he said with what I gleaned from others later that day, I wrote the following in my journal:

"About 2:00 p.m., with Paulsen in the chair, the item regarding the new editor came up. Bill J's retirement was voted, with many nice things said about his tenure. Attention then turned to the matter of his successor. Much discussion ensued, centered around the reason why Roy Adams had been bypassed. 'Why didn't you consult with the regional leaders?' one or two of the African American committee members wanted to know. To which Paulsen explained that the AR is a world entity, though located in North America.

Nothing bad was said about Bill K, but many questions were asked about the process. Paulsen for his part, unable to bring forward the matter of my age (having been advised that that could open up the church to legal liability), was left with no solid reason for preferring Knott."

Later in the evening, Harold Lee called me and added to the story, which I also jotted down, as follows:

"Harold said he really did not want to confront the president in public; but when he saw Paulsen's bungling while introducing the item, the feeling built up in him that he had to address it. As he tried to make his point, Paulsen somehow felt he had to defend himself against the intimation of racism. His decision had not been based on such considerations. 'I did not introduce the matter of race,' Harold said in response. 'I'm talking about competence and the unwritten rules of succession. Bill Johnsson called Roy to the present job, and they'd been working together for 16 years. Bill K came 8 years ago. The one has a doctorate in theology, the other a doctorate in American history. Go figure.'

Harold then moved to refer the item for further consideration, and that the vote to refer be taken by secret ballot. (The idea to refer, he said, had occurred to him literally as he headed to the microphone.) Paulsen tried to haggle over the motion to refer, prompting Harold (a parliamentary rules sleuth) to remind him that the motion to refer entertains no debate. The motion carried, Harold said, 58 to 46. Harold commended (GC education director) Garland Dulan and Roscoe Howard for the speeches they made, given their positions. Garland, he said, made the strongest speech of all."

The vote to refer had been heavily influenced by union presidents, Harold told me later, many of whom came to him afterwards to commend him for "doing the right thing." "But none of them had the courage to step up to the mike," he lamented. "It's a failure of courage."

Later that evening, Howard dropped by my room, and reiterated several of the things Harold had earlier shared. The strongest speech came from Dulan, he said, who approached the issue from the standpoint of educational assessment, questioning the homework Paulsen and the others had done before coming to their conclusion. Dulan posed several questions, each of which sent Paulsen squirming, Howard said. At the end of his remarks, before returning to his seat, Dulan said: "Mr. Chairman, I don't think you answered any of my questions."

Roscoe said that when Harold Lee moved to refer, Paulsen asked: "Is there a second?" Rosa Banks (an African American), sitting beside him as the recording secretary, promptly said: "Second." Roscoe had never before seen such a thing on such a sensitive issue. It indicated to me the anger that Paulsen's action had generated in the African American Adventist community. Had he decided in my favor, everything would have been on his side: protocol, logic, the unwritten rules of succession, common sense, etc. But it was clear that, for whatever reasons, he was dead set on keeping me from the position. He'd doggedly stuck to his guns, and things had blown up in his face.

I was stunned at the surprising turn of events. And in my prayer the following Sabbath back in Washington, I told the Lord how utterly amazed I still was over the events of the week. *"My interpretation of the developments,"* I wrote in my journal, *"is that they were a rebuke both to me and to Paulsen. I think the humiliation I've been through has not totally been without cause. But I also think that God especially intervened to rebuke the palpable unfairness and injustice of Paulsen's action."*

During my reflections, my mind often turned to Paulsen's indication to me that he and his vice presidents (Lowell Cooper, Mark Finley, Jerry Karst, Eugene Hsu, Armando Miranda, Pardon Mwansa, Mike Ryan, Ella Simmons, Ted Wilson) had constituted the initial search committee for a new editor. And I got to wondering: *Were they all present at the meeting where the action was taken to put Knott's name forward? Did they all concur? Did anyone as much as raise a question on the matter of basic fairness?* If not, then the outcome at Loma Linda stood as a rebuke to them, as well.

"*I stand amazed at these developments,*" I wrote that Sabbath morning, April 15. "*I didn't suspect God would do it this way. And if I seem to be repeating myself in these journal entries, it's because I'm utterly overwhelmed that God would intervene in this fashion.*"

The previous Wednesday, after Paulsen had sent word that Bill K and I should not be present for the afternoon session, I'd gone back to the hotel after lunch, as I said earlier. I prayed before taking a rest, and as I awoke, I also prayed—kneeling in bed under the covers in the cold room (I'd turned the air-conditioning system down for resting, as is my custom). I can remember how alone I felt there, how helpless to sway events, and how bleak the future looked for me. In that dark time, the words of the psalmist spoke to my deep need:

"Hear my cry, O God; listen to my prayer.
From the ends of the earth I call to you,
I call as my heart grows faint;
lead me to the rock that is higher than I" (Psa. 61:1, 2).
"Find rest, O my soul, in God alone; my hope comes from him.
He alone is my rock and my salvation; he is my fortress, I will not be shaken.
My salvation and my honor depend on God; he is my mighty rock, my refuge" (Psa. 62:5-7).

With those meetings over, my discomfort with remaining at the *Adventist Review* office had become so intense that I began exploring various alternatives. An opening at the (Columbia Union) *Visitor* was discussed; and I talked to two leaders in the GC complex about possible openings in their departments—the kind of thing I've not had to do in all my ministry. *"So I am brought to this,"* I journaled, *"It is a humiliating time for me. But—at least for the time being—God has drastically changed the outlook. I can't help wondering what I'd be writing this morning if Paulsen's plans had carried the day. Wow! I can't get over what God has done!"*

The Tuesday after my return from Loma Linda, Paulsen called me into his office for a chat (he'd already spoken to Bill K—I was always second, if not third). "Roy, I thought I should sit down with you after what happened [at Loma Linda]," he began, "especially since you and I have always had an easy working relationship. You have taken events in an almost stoical manner. I assume you've heard about what happened at Loma Linda."

I assured him I had. "Bill J briefed me," I said.

He appeared quite shaken by what had transpired, describing it to me as a "bruising" experience. (And given his choice of words, I couldn't help noticing that a small bandage covered a bruise-like scar on his nose as we spoke, as if to symbolize the recent skirmish). He was disappointed that he was made out to have racist motives in the choice he'd put forward, noting that "all six—and the only six" who went to the microphone tended directly or indirectly to characterize him as racially insensitive. "As I know my heart before God," he said as if under oath, "I'm not."

Bill K is apparently considering a move, he told me; and so he pled with me to stay. "We need you. If you both leave, the Review would be in grave difficulty. I can understand why Bill Knott might want to leave," he said, "feeling that he's been rejected. But as I explained to him, this was not a rejection of him; it was simply the body saying to us: Step back; do some more reflection."

Still, he'd told Bill that he should not expect him "to bring his name back." "Back to the drawing board," he told him, "means back to the drawing board." "Not that it won't happen," he was careful to add, "but I wanted him to be clear on that"

In regard to process, the president said to me, he would involve the division presidents earlier this time, and would run things by the NAD union presidents when he met with them in August (2006), since a sizeable part of AR's ministry is in North America.

Before our meeting ended, he again brought up the qualification of the AR editor in chief, among other things stressing that the person should hold to a theologically centrist position, and *"should reflect the culture of the church naturally and from the inside."* The whole process will open up again, he said, and they'll be looking outside the magazine.

If Paulsen was not prepared to bring Knott's name back, it was also clear to me (without him actually having to say it) that he wasn't about to put mine forward either. After all, it was clear to me that part of his reasons for having Bill J delay his retirement by several years—and prolong his stay as chief editor of the magazine—was the troubling, unwritten line of succession element staring him in the face. By the way things are supposed to work in the church, I was next in line, and it would seem that his own inclination, strengthened (I suspected) by powerful people in the church, combined to thwart what would otherwise have been the normal course of events.

That had come through clearly to me a year earlier, when he'd first talked to me about the editor-in-chief position. His statement to me then was that I was not centrist enough; that my writing had "ruffled some feathers." An editor of the church's flagship magazine, he'd said then, could not be seen as taking sides either on the right or on the left. His words had led me to believe that something I'd written (or my writings in general) must have offended someone (or a few people) with powerful (perhaps financial) clout in the church. Perhaps to these people, and also to him, I did not "reflect the culture of the church naturally and from the inside."

There had to be some "program" operating in the background of his head, away from public view, that was affecting the elder. At a retirement function for Harold Lee on May 21, several weeks after the Loma Linda meetings, my wife and I happened to be sitting at the same table with former GC president Neal C Wilson. Without any prompting on my part, he brought up the editor situation, expressing surprise that "the long-held tradition of seniority had not been followed." That was interesting talk, and I wanted to hear more from this veteran Adventist administrator. But as he took breath to continue, the MC's voice came over the loud-speaker and brought our tête-à-tête to an abrupt end, and we never returned to the subject.

Evidently, Neal Wilson was not alone in his surprise at the doggedness of the then current president. A few weeks after the Loma Linda meetings, an official who was in the room as Paulsen had met with the division presidents told me that when Knott's name was presented by Paulsen, the division presidents were taken aback. That person said that at that very moment he could have told Paulsen that the nomination was doomed. Paulsen himself, however, did not see it coming. At the meeting, three division presidents spoke glowingly of my work in their territories; and although the official speaking to me did not name them, I believe the speakers certainly would have included Laurie Evans, then president of the South Pacific Division—a straight talker, and a prince of a gentleman.

Looking back on the Loma Linda meetings, the official told me, Paulsen felt that his division colleagues had let him down; that they did not support him. He felt that if just one or two of them had risen in defense of the nomination, that it would have carried the day. But none went to the microphone. The Regional presidents, to mention another group, saw through what was happening, the official told me. Paulsen all along had been presenting Bill K and me as equals. If that was so, the Regional presidents reasoned, then why would Paulsen deliberately choose the shorter-serving Caucasian candidate? It led them to the conclusion that somehow race was a factor.

That may well have been the case. But nailing down racial bias is sometimes as difficult as pinning jello to a wall. To cite the perceptive words of two of my former colleagues, "Selfishness, racial prejudice, pride, abuse, envy, and greed will simply find a new, more politically correct form of expression as social climates change" (Chantal and

Gerald Klingbeil, *Adventist World,* Nov 2011, p. 19).

My suspicion has always been that powerful, behind-the-scenes forces in the church influenced the process. Over the years, I have been amazed by the amount of influence such people wield. I remember that in a meeting with *Review* editors when he was president, Robert Folkenberg expressed his regret that we'd published a news article on an inter-collegiate sports event, in which a Seventh-day Adventist team that had refused to play on Sabbath ended up winning. Someone had called him over the weekend, he said, complaining about the publication of the piece (because of the church's frown on intermural sports). "Let me get this straight," I remember saying to him (with incredulity in my voice as we discussed the issue), "the person who complained to you was able to reach you at home on the week-end? They had your personal telephone number?" Sensing the drift of my query, he followed up with a few generalizations, and quickly vacated the dicey subject.

People in the church with money "have access," just as in the political world. A single call in the night from one of them can affect a leader's thinking, and send a little guy like me out to pasture in a hurry. And as I sized up the president, I got the sense that something like that had to lie behind his dogged opposition to my candidacy. (I will touch again on this later.)

Even though I talked precious little about my situation with folk around me, I had occasion to share that last hunch with a trusted colleague in the GC complex, who added an interesting tidbit of his own. About two or three years earlier, he said, a person "high up" in the GC hierarchy (he didn't give a name) had mentioned that the powers that be have some strikes against me because of my theology, though they won't say so in public. It went as far back, he said, as the time I was being called to the *Review*, when someone on the committee (as I said in an earlier chapter) charged that I'd written for *Spectrum*. Although that was a false charge, he said, the stigma stuck.

His observations brought back to mind a brief encounter I'd had with (then GC vice president) Ted Wilson. Word had reached me that in the lead up to the Loma Linda meetings he'd chaired (or had been on) a committee, in which he'd argued against my candidacy for editor because of my position on the human nature of Christ. So when we accidentally met one day in the GC lobby, I confronted him with the rumor I'd heard. What aspect of my position on Christ's human nature did he find troubling? And in his typically blunt manner he told me: "You hold to a pre-lapsarian view, and I cannot vote for someone with that position to become editor of the *Review.*" [In theology, the pre-lapsarian position on the nature of Christ holds that Christ took the nature of Adam before he fell (that is, before he lapsed) into sin. The post-lapsarian view is that Jesus took fallen human nature (that is, human nature after Adam had lapsed into sin.)]

What would I have gained by arguing with him after the fact? But I was saddened that such a responsible leader in the church could have been so reckless on a matter that involved someone else's career. For, after all, he was not basing his charge on a speech I'd given, where a person could have misheard or misunderstood what I might have said. No, he was basing his allegation on something I had written. Written! So that one may go back and read the chapter or the paragraph or the sentence again, and make doubly sure!

So what had I written? In my book on the nature of Christ, after a protracted assessment of the pre-lapsarian/post-lapsarian issue over two chapters, I came down on the side of what I considered the position of Ellen G. White, and wrote, as follows: "We may conclude, therefore, that so far as Ellen G. White was concerned, the incarnate Christ was neither exactly like Adam before the Fall nor exactly like us. In other words, He was unique" (*The Nature of Christ*—Review & Herald, 1994, p. 69). I will leave it to the reader to characterize such gross (and apparently willful) misrepresentation on the part of such a high-placed leader in the church.

But now all that was water under the bridge. The unexpected developments at the Spring Meeting were behind us. And the question now was: what happens next.

CHAPTER 14

Second-guessing, Recrimination, and another Search Committee

BETWEEN THE LOMA Linda meetings in the spring of 2006 and Annual Council in the fall, the political wheels vis-à-vis the *Adventist Review* editorship kept turning. It was a time of reflection, second-guessing and, in some respects, recrimination.

I left for British Columbia the day after my post Loma Linda talk with Paulsen. While in travel, I missed a call from Bill J; and when we finally connected the following day (Thursday April 20), he shared his impression that Bill K seemed to be on his way out, and he wanted to alert me that soon we should begin the difficult process of looking for a replacement. During the course of our conversation, he told me that Bill K seemed to be blaming him for the outcome at Loma Linda. He was charging that when Bill J had briefed the staff from Loma Linda on developments regarding the position of editor, he had repeatedly emphasized that "the two candidates were equal in qualification and gifts." That was a mistake, Bill K now claimed. Rather, there ought to have been an assessment that clearly came down on his side as the superior candidate, thus eliminating any confusion.

Johnsson was at a loss to understand Knott's logic, since he (Johnsson) was merely repeating sentiments from Paulsen's meeting with the presidents. (My own interpretation of what Knott meant, however, was that Johnsson, in his briefing of Paulsen, might have conveyed the impression that his two associates were, indeed, equal; and that that was what caused Paulsen to present the case the way he did at Spring Meeting, leading to the outcome that ensued.) It was "a very strange and unpleasant conversation," Johnsson told me, "and I was glad when it was over."

"How things can change!" I wrote in my journal that Saturday evening in my room at the lodge on the Hope campground there in British Columbia. *"My mouth is still wide open in astonishment at all these developments. What I've always suspected in Bill K is now clear before my face. Only now can it be clearly seen how badly he wanted the job, how totally unconcerned he was for the feelings of others, and how completely insincere were his sentiments the afternoon Bill J met with him and me following Paulsen's talk with both of us that morning. In that afternoon meeting, Bill K was generous in his praise of me—how the staff respects me, how they all look to me for wise counsel, etc. He has a way with words, and they flowed freely. But now I know what then I could only suspect: It was all an act.... Now that he didn't get what he'd been feverishly striving for, he's picking up his marbles and abandoning the game. Incredible!"*

The following Friday (April 28), Bill J called me into his office and said: "Roy, perhaps I already said this to you—and if I didn't, I should have: I want to compliment you on the way you have comported yourself these past four weeks" (meaning during the time since I knew that Bill K's name had been chosen in place of mine). It was a genuine compliment, of course, and I took it as such. But it did remind me of what Paulsen had said about my response being "stoical." And it made me wonder what they'd been expecting of me—that I would freak out, perhaps? Throw a tantrum?

Meanwhile a search committee had been formed, hand-picked by Paulsen: Orville Parchment (chair), Jerry Karst, Mike Ryan, Ella Simmons, and Armando Miranda. All, except Parchment, were vice-presidents and, as such, had been members of the original (larger) search committee that Paulsen had months before described to me.

During the course of their deliberations, the committee came up with five names: Roy Gane (of Andrews University), Les Pollard (then of Loma Linda University), Angel Rodriguez (then director of the GC's Biblical Research Institute), Bill Knott, and Roy Adams.

On Monday, May 22, I received a letter from the committee's chair. The committee, the letter said, would like me to write out my vision for *Adventist Review/Adventist World;* outline how I plan to market the magazines; and provide two samples of my best articles.

The following journal entry came after that development (and here I alter a few specifics in the entry to protect the identity of the individual concerned—it is that sensitive):

*"**Monday, May 22.** While I was reflecting on a response to the committee's letter, and within an hour of receiving it, an official from a racial minority working at the GC dropped by my office. He wanted to share with me how he'd experienced the very thing I'm going through now. Told me of how Paulsen, when he came to office, asked a certain high GC official slated for retirement to stay on two more years [does that ring a bell?]. When it came time to elect that official's replacement, my visitor's name was placed in nomination with all the others. When the committee met, they asked Paulsen for his preference. Paulsen gave a name; and within 10 minutes that person was voted.*

The following day, he said, the committee came to elect the next ranking officer of that department, and some official asked him for a resume. He gave it; but now believes they had no intention of electing him—it was only window dressing. From that day he's taken the position of never again submitting his resume. If the committee knows his work, let them elect him. If they don't, then let them turn to someone else. He doesn't want to be used again.

That was uncanny stuff, coming less than an hour after I'd received Parchment's letter. And it settled me in the view that I would respectfully refuse to submit the documents the search committee was requesting."

I drafted a strongly-worded response to the search committee's letter. "I was surprised by the request," it said in part, and "dumb-founded that after nearly 18 years as an editor at the *Adventist Review*," I am being asked "by a search committee to submit two of my best articles" for their examination. (The rest of the letter only got stronger—and I don't want to reproduce it here.)

When I shared the draft with a trusted friend in the complex, he laughed. I fully understand where you're coming from, he said, "but it's too strong, and it can come back to hurt you." He was right, and I decided not to send it after all. Which is why I restricted myself in the above quote to only a few of its less pungent lines.

The letter that actually went read (in part), as follows:

"May 25, 2006
Dear Orville:
I consented to leave my name on the search committee list for editor-in-chief of *Adventist Review/Adventist World*. This means that if chosen and elected, I will give the assignment my best shot, under God. That has always been my approach to service in the church, and will continue.

But as I mentioned to you on the phone when you passed on Elder Paulsen's inquiry as to whether I'd consent to leave my name in nomination, so to speak, I'm not seeking the office. Nor have I ap-plied for it. Accordingly, I think it would be inappropriate to comply with the particular requests contained in your letter. I've been with the *Review* running on 18 years now, and been intimately involved in all its dreams and ventures during that period. All these things are matters of public record.

I suspect that in preparing to deal with the many candidates that might be on your search list, you designed a one-size-fits-all instru-ment, without thinking how it might impact any one candidate. That's quite understandable. As you might imagine, however, this has been a very humbling—not to say humiliating—period for me; and I'm sure your committee would not knowingly want to exacerbate that situation.

Cordially yours in service,

Roy Adams"

Moments after receiving my letter, Parchment dropped by to see me. He'd tried to dissuade the committee from proceeding in the direction it did, he said. "At this level," he'd told the members, "you either know the person or you don't. You don't ask them to go through these exercises." But they had insisted, he said. He wanted me to know that he fully understood where I was coming from, and asked my permission to share the letter with the committee—a permission I readily granted, of course (since, after all, I'd written the letter *for* the committee). As it turned out, Parchment had also shared my letter with Paulsen, who called later that day to say how much he has "admired [my] spirit throughout this period," though he knows it had to be difficult for me. What I said in the letter was right on, he said; he fully agreed with me; and he just wanted me to know that—and to know how much he admires the way I've responded to all that had happened.

So was he undercutting his own search committee? I didn't quite know. But it was one more element in the puzzle of a president trying to navigate his way through a sensitive and ever changing terrain, while under some kind of external duress, a specter that onlookers, near and far, found difficult to fathom. One colleague, returning from an itinerary in Asia, dropped by to touch base with me in the afternoon of May 25. He told me that wherever he went—Japan, Singapore, etc.—"people are asking: Whatever happened at Loma Linda?" There is great puzzlement out there, he said; and he added one interesting detail he'd received from someone within the GC administration in a position to know (whom he named). The person told him that as the Spring Meeting took up the *Review* editor item, Bill K was in a nearby room, waiting to be called in at the right moment.

Thus, as it turned out, Loma Linda proved painful for both of us.

One of us found himself in an adjoining room, awaiting the moment of a coronation that never came. The other was sitting alone in a hotel room three miles away, facing what he saw as an uncertain future. It was a stark picture that summarized for me the extraordinary pathos of that eventful day.

By the end of June, three of the five candidates the search committee had in its sights were showing signs of disinterest, one administrator casually told me as we crossed paths in the GC lobby one day. Les Pollard, he said, had removed his name; Roy Gane (he was hearing) had no current plans to leave Andrews University; and Angel Rodriguez was not interested. Rodriguez had himself shared that detail with me, and if his name still appeared on the final list, it could be that he'd been persuaded to leave it there for cosmetic reasons. Knott, he speculated, had probably received assurances from "someone" that his name was coming back, and that this time it was going to pass; which was probably why he'd turned down job offers from Carolina Conference, Andrews University, and the Ellen G White Estate.

That last tidbit meshed with what I'd noticed about Bill in the days and weeks preceding that conversation—a hardly disguised spring in the steps, and an absence of the moroseness that had gripped him following Loma Linda.

On July 5, Parchment called to inform me that his search committee had completed its work and was recommending three names to Paulsen, and that my name was one of them. (Paulsen would take the names to the North American Division union presidents' meeting a few weeks later and, in concert with then North American Division president Don Schneider, would urge in favor of Knott. The two leaders left the meeting feeling confident they had their man this time.)

And they were correct. The die, in effect, had been cast, and the remaining weeks of summer and early fall were simply a period of waiting for the official Annual Council confirmation.

CHAPTER 15

Maneuvers and Intrigues on the Way to Annual Council

AS OCTOBER CAME, the month for Annual Council, the final wheels began to turn. And I recorded the following in my journal:

"*10/3/06. Paulsen has just left my office. Informed me that Bill K's name will be presented to Annual Council. They'd thought about it long and hard, he said. Finally, they came up with 5 names, with two dropping out. The final three, he said, were Bill K, Angel Rodriguez, and myself. He'd convened a meeting of GC officers and North American Division union presidents, and the secret-ballot vote between Knott and me came out 14/14. But the union presidents had indicated to him in the end that they'd support whomever he presented. And he was prepared to present Bill's name.*"

Without any solicitation on my part, I'd been hearing from different sources about the various votes that had been taken on the editor question, and after a while found it rather confusing to follow. What came through clearly, however, was that Paulsen was desperately working the various groups in an effort to cover himself and secure the vote he wanted. One union president told me, for example—referring to that 14/14 vote Paulsen told me about—that there actually had been two votes. The first time around, Rodriguez got 3, and Bill and I tied. In the second vote, I came in with 14 and Bill K with

13—something that shocked Paulsen, he said.

But three union presidents had been participating via conference call; and when that second vote was taken, one of them, for some reason, was off line. It was his vote, coming to Paulsen later, that tied it. But the curious thing, said the union president talking to me, was that weeks earlier when they'd discussed the editor issue among themselves as union presidents, that particular person had been one of those strongly rooting for me. Which led him to the suspicion, he said, that that president's vote might have been coached.

Thus with a tied vote, Paulsen simply selected Bill K as his candidate. So when he convened the pre-annual council meeting of the General Conference (GC) and division officers, one high official told me, he did not ask for a new vote. Instead, referring to the tie vote in question, he simply informed the group that he'd selected Bill K, and asked for their support.

Thus at his October 3 meeting with me in my office, Paulsen informed me (as I wrote in my journal later that day) that *"he'd be presenting Bill K's name to the council, and he wanted me to know that ahead of time. (He'd already spoken to BJ and BK—I was always last.) This perhaps explains Bill K's unusual pleasantness when I arrived at work this morning. Things are working out exactly as I suspected they would."*

During our staff meeting on October 4, Bill J shared with us the action of the *Adventist Review* board vis-à-vis the position of the editor. He said that after giving the board a description of the selection process that had been followed in choosing the new editor, Paulsen had put the matter to a vote. "It carried unanimously," Bill J said. According to the minutes of that meeting, those present were: Jan Paulsen (chair), Bill J (secretary), Robert Kyte, Armando Miranda, Pardon Mwansa, Steve Rose, Charles Sandefur, Don Schneider, Robert Smith, and Ted Wilson. (In Bill J's description of the vote at that AR board meeting lies a puzzle that I've tried to grapple with, but may never understand. Match, if you will, the names of those present at that board meeting with Johnsson's statement: "It carried unanimously.")

The next day came the following e-mail from Bill J:

"Colleagues,

"Here's an update on developments:

"Last evening ADCOM met and voted to pass on the AR Board recommendation to the Annual Council—that is, that Bill Knott be appointed as editor-in-chief, effective January 1 [2007].

"Pastor Paulsen discussed with me the matter of timing. He is planning to have our [Adventist World] report come on Sunday morning, or, if it can't be fitted in, early Sunday afternoon. The election of the new editor will come immediately after the AW report."

Apparently cocksure of the outcome, Bill J continued:

"I leave for Dubai Wednesday, October 11 and return October 25. Bill [Knott] will be in charge of the office while I am away. He may call a planning meeting during that period; I have encouraged him to do so.

"The protracted period of uncertainty at last is coming to a close. I commend you for the professional manner in which you have gone about your work, and see good days ahead for the AR and AW.

"Best wishes,

Bill"

That afternoon (October 4), Bill J came to my office to tell me of an encounter he'd just had. He'd gone out to lunch with some colleagues from the complex, and someone had confronted him about the editor situation. "Is it something you said to Paulsen that has caused him to turn away from Roy to Bill?" That rumor is going around in some circles in the building, the person told him. The charge had hurt him keenly, Bill J told me, wiping tears from his eyes. "Especially as the facts are just the opposite," he said.

"At this time in my life," I journaled in the wake of these developments, *"God seems so utterly silent! How I pray that another door might open in this area (so Celia's work would not be interrupted)! Nothing seems even close to opening. And just about every avenue*

my mind runs to is controlled by the very two men who are the prime movers of this very process—Paulsen and Schneider. I seem to be in a bind here."

Continuing with some personal reflections, I wrote:

"It's not, I think, a question of humility here—it's humiliation. You've been at this now for 18 years, and someone with less than half that time on the job… has been made your boss, to put it bluntly. Something has died within me. The enthusiasm is gone. As if the wind's been blown out of my sails. As if I can no longer put 100% of myself into the effort—indeed, I feel as if I no longer have 100% to give. My mind's no longer fully in it. I feel as if I can no longer undertake strenuous missions for AR/AW. I feel as if I can never go to a Black gathering again and ask them to subscribe to the AR."

That last remark about feeling an inability to promote the magazine in the Black community in the future gets, I think, to the core of what was eating me up during this period. As I've said before, my heart was not skipping beats in anticipation of becoming editor of *Adventist Review/Adventist world*. I was not yearning for the position. I've always thought it unseemly to push myself forward, and have despised the scramble for position and power that has afflicted altogether too many in the church. Come election time, a strange intoxication seems to descend upon us; a vicious, dog-eat-dog mentality. I find it unseemly, even stupid at times. Stupid in the sense of its comparative worthlessness at the end of the day in this miniscule pond of ours, let alone the wider scheme of things in the larger world.

Nevertheless, the situation being what it was, people repeatedly would bring up the matter of Bill J's successor as I traveled over the years. And however much the subject embarrassed me, I did get a sense as to how much it meant to these inquirers—especially those in the African American community—for me to achieve the position. It eventually brought me to the place where I felt as if I stood in their place; that my victory would be their victory, my triumph their triumph. And so in the wake of the new developments, I had the strange feeling that I'd let them down somehow. And, equally important, that the church, by passing over my name, had rejected *them*. However difficult to understand, I felt the burden of those dashed expectations not so much for my own sake (if you can believe it), but for theirs.

The editorship item came up Sunday, October 8; and from the get-go it was clear that Paulsen would have his wish. With Ted Wilson in the chair, several council members spoke, mostly Blacks—and all African Americans. Gina Brown of Washington Adventist University was one of them, speaking forcefully and with passion. And Ivan Warden of the Ellen G White Estate gave a strong mince-no-words speech. But given who controlled the chair, the passionate appeals from the likes of Brown and Warden were no match for the one-sentence gem presented by the director of the GC's Geo-science Research Institute (based at Loma Linda). He took to the floor to say that "Whenever I receive my copy of the *Adventist Review*, the first article I turn to is Bill Knott's editorial." That was all he said—and with the chair on his side, that was all he needed to say. (The statement was ludicrous, of course. After all, every editor when they travel somehow runs into folk who swear that that particular editor's article is always the "first one" they turn to. That's why the learned gentleman's remarks, which he waited a good while in line to deliver, were so curious.)

During the debate on the floor of the council, charges of racism were leveled, however indirectly, with Paulsen protesting his innocence, invoking God (in a sense) as his witness. That led me to think: *How can we not believe him? After all, he is a man of integrity. He perhaps believes completely in what he's saying—that his position is not based on race.*

But what it's actually based on is perhaps a little more complicated. Perhaps, in the words of certain commercial firms—airlines, in particular—the church has what we might call its "preferred customers"—or, in this case, its "preferred candidates" for certain offices. And it would seem that one can establish those criteria clearly in mind (whatever they are), and philosophically distinguish them from racism. Not everything is easy to nail down and, as I indicated earlier, racism is one of the most difficult.

I myself have never thought of racism as the primary motive influencing Paulsen's actions. But I've always suspected the presence of external forces—wealthy people in the church, for example, with strong, "conservative" opinions, and willing to use their giving power as leverage for their positions and views. An editor of the church's premier magazine, with strong opinions of their own, would very likely arouse the ire of such folk, who usually are not shy about wielding their enormous clout with the powers that be. They have the ability to reach a GC president on his home or personal cell phone in the night and on the weekend. It is the motives of such stealth individuals that are hard to smoke out. I hinted at that in the Folkenberg snippet in a previous chapter. And if the motivation of such people is tinged with racism, then Paulsen could vociferously deny such attitudes in himself, with the end result being the same.

Some of us have noticed a certain administrative pattern, when it comes to electing minority individuals to some of the highest offices in the church.

Don King (who is Black) was executive secretary of the Alberta Conference when the conference president accepted a call to another field. The unspoken rule of succession should have seen him become president, but the vote did not go that way. Instead, he remained at his post as secretary. In the wake of Folkenberg's resignation as GC president in February, 1999, and as the committee whittled down the nominations to succeed him to just two names—Jan Paulsen and Calvin Rock, former GC vice president Ken Mittleider took to the floor and threw a barrel of cold water on Rock's candidacy by stressing the critical importance of overseas mission service for a GC president, something that Rock did not have. Many believe that that speech affected the vote, tipping the scale against Rock. And, to an extent, that was probably true.

But there was something that happened in regard to Rock's name that not many people know about. Before Mittleider's speech, there had been a break in the proceedings. During that break, an official who was present told me, the NAD convened a meeting of its officers and union presidents so as to come up with a united strategy going forward. During the special confab, when it appeared that support was building for Rock's name, (then) NAD president Alfred C. McClure spoke up: "There are wealthy people in the church," he said, "who will withhold their support if Rock becomes GC president." "I heard that with my own ears," the official told me. That warning, the official thinks, given the administrative pattern that seems pervasive in this church, was a powerful, silent factor that affected the vote on the committee when it later reconvened.

In March 2006, after the Andrews University board forced the resignation of University president Niels-Erik Andreasen, Calvin Rock (then recently retired) was invited to serve as interim president, pending the result of a search committee and the installation of a permanent replacement. But the thought of a Black person serving as president of the prestigious institution, even in an interim capacity, was apparently so alarming that a series of "political" maneuvers were initiated by some of the highest powers that be in church, leading to the reinstatement of Andreasen as president.

R. Clifford Jones was associate dean of Andrews University Theological Seminary when the post of dean became vacant in 2013; but the mantle, undoubtedly for the usual reasons, did not fall on him, marking the second time he'd been passed over for the deanship.

So at every one of our committee, board, and constituency meetings, certain factors (usually unspoken) lurk in the background, constantly affecting how people think and vote. It's a pattern. There's a saying in the African American community that when pitted against a Caucasian candidate for any job or office, "You have to be twice as good as them to get half what they have."

In his general remarks to the 2006 Annual Council, introducing the discussion of the editor item, Paulsen had indicated that some of those approached by the search committee had asked that their names be withdrawn. This prompted (then) Allegheny East Conference president Charles Cheatham to ask during the discussion time whether

Roy Adams was one of those who'd withdrawn their names. Paulsen's response was that it would not be proper for him to go into such details.

It was a particularly misleading answer—even deliberately deceptive. For it clearly left the impression in Cheatham's mind (and in the minds of others) that I *might have been* one of those who'd made such a request. And not knowing the facts, Cheatham found himself unable to pursue whatever argument he had in mind to make, and simply sat down after the exchange. The president's cunning answer had shut him up. It would have been entirely appropriate for the president to say: "No, Adams was not one of those." It would have betrayed no one's confidence. But, as he suspected, it would have brought his arbitrary selection into bolder relief before the council, and he did not relish that.

The motion carried. And Bill Knott was now the new man at the helm—effective January 1, 2007.

One thing to remember about these annual meetings is that the GC administration controls the agenda, and virtually controls the outcome. Typically, printed items appearing on the floor for action come with a slew of abbreviations at the top of the page or document, indicating the various committees or groups through which the particular item had passed. And the psychological effect on the regular committee member is for them to conclude that if all these groups and committees have already cleared the matter, who am I to oppose it at this stage? So unless it's an item that directly affects the budget or some other critical aspect of their own local field, they are ready to say "Aye" to whatever they think the top leaders want. Moreover, it's no secret that many aspiring leaders on the committee understand that their future rise in the ecclesiastical power structure could be dependent on their ability to toe the GC administrative line, whatever that may be, and not ask difficult questions.

In the days following the vote, several members of the council came by my office to talk, to encourage, to pray. Dan Jackson; Don King; Harold Baptiste; Saustin Mfune (then president of the Malawi

Union Mission); Fred Kinsey (just to squeeze my hand); Claude Sabot (who also, as an associate GC secretary, brought a request from Southern Asia Pacific Division president Alberto Gulfan about my becoming education director of his division—which I declined, with deep appreciation.) Jackson had taken on Paulsen in earlier meetings, he told me, and felt any opposition to his choice for editor was hopeless, once it got to Annual Council—which is why he did not speak during the discussion on the item. Others made calls to me, or sent letters or emails, the strongest email coming from someone who'd both interned and worked as a regular at the magazine.

This last individual, Andy Nash, even went on a *Spectrum* blog to express his outrage. Adams, he wrote in a loaded comment, "isn't political—isn't constantly trying to position himself, doesn't 'kiss up and kick down.' He treats everyone with respect, whether above him or below him. There were times when I saw an issue differently than Adams did. But I never felt demeaned by Adams, and I never saw him demean other staff members or production staff at the publishing house."

You have to have worked in our office for a while to fully understand the implications of those sentiments and the message behind them. And although I felt totally unworthy of many of the kind things Nash said about me in the piece, I understood his general point perfectly.

His most cogent observation came, as I recall, toward the end. "The fact that Adams would have been the first black editor in the *Review*'s 157-year history would have been a bonus—an important first for a church that's never been on the leading edge of racial unity." (Andy Nash, in a *Spectrum* blog, October 13, 2006.)

Shredding all vanity, as best I could, I tried objectively to see the validity of that last point. If Paulsen would have said that he'd been visited by an angel in the night, that he'd received some divine vision or intelligence to proceed the way he did, I think I'd have understood completely. But he made no such claims. Which left me baffled that a person of such keen intellect could have missed an opportunity of this magnitude, an opportunity to make history—an opportunity that, given current trends, probably will not present itself again in at least half a century.

After the U.S. civil rights movement and actions by the Supreme Court forced Adventists (among other religious groups) to change the way they did business, it was as if some unwritten understanding pre-scribed a "thus far and no further" stipulation. And it appears that the editorship of the church's flagship journal was a golden plum to be carefully guarded. After all, it boasted the likes of James White, Uriah Smith, and other luminaries of Adventist history. Not a role for "com-moners," but for persons who (to use Paulsen's words) "reflect the culture of the church naturally and from the inside."

Adventists are good on doctrine, on theology; but they often fall flat when it comes to ethics and justice. Over the years since that editorship election, I've not discussed the matter often, but where ap-propriate I've tried to explain to people that even though these things happened to me, I'm able to push away from the subjective elements and make an objective assessment of the whole situation. I've always maintained that I can sit on a jury deliberating a case involving my own wife, my own son or daughter, or some other close relative, and still reach an impartial decision—though if it came to reporting a guilty verdict to the judge, I would have to recuse myself; for at that point, I suspect, family ties and sentiments would overwhelm my objectivity. But up to that point, I can handle it. Drilled into me from the start under the British educational system was the discipline of ap-proaching an issue with complete dispassion, following the evidence wherever it leads.

With that attitude, as I've tried to explain to people, I was able to focus on the developments surrounding the election of a new edi-tor virtually as an objective bystander—as if I were not involved at all—and assess it purely on the basis of fairness and justice. I've dis-covered that it's a concept many have difficulty grasping, let alone appreciating. Blank stares would greet me each time I've tried to ar-ticulate it, as if I were speaking a foreign language.

Perhaps the same basic point might come through clearer as I put it in writing for the first time. (Again, like Paul, I speak as a fool, and ask you to forgive my bluntness.) I can hardly believe I'm doing this— I of all people! But here's the illustration—it's turned upside down and inside out, so you've got to pay attention to get the point:

A Caucasian person has been working at the *Adventist Review* for 18 years, laboring night and day for the success of the publication. They've carried the load in peaceful times and during times of crisis. They've been in charge of the office on a multitude of occasions, when the editor in chief had been traveling or been on furlough. During those times, no crisis had arisen that was not effectively handled; there had never been a complaint from any of the staff when the editor returned. In every such instance, all the operations of the office had gone smoothly and without a hitch.

This Caucasian person was not the best writer in the world, but they did a fairly decent job, appreciated by the majority of the magazine's readers. And by the time it came to the election of a new editor, this Caucasian associate editor had had at least four books published under his name (with three others simultaneously in publication at the time); and held a PhD in theology for more than two decades, his doctoral dissertation grappling with the critical subject of the doctrine of the sanctuary in the Adventist Church. This Caucasian associate editor had been several years a pastor; and after teaching classes at Andrews University Theological Seminary (while doing post graduate studies) had done a six-year stint of overseas service as a professor of theology at a division-run seminary, during which time (through extension schools and other appointments), he had had opportunity to interact with students, teachers, and the general Adventist membership in at least eight Asian countries.

The other associate is Black. An excellent writer, he'd served as a church pastor for several years, and he was about nine years on the AR staff when it came time to elect a new editor. Six months or so earlier, the Black associate had received his PhD in American History, with a dissertation on Hannah More, an American missionary to

Liberia, who came to accept the Seventh-day Adventist message. This Black associate, at the time of the election for editor, was without any overseas mission service, or any books published under his name.

Given the two sets of qualification just described, what do you think would be the chances of that Black associate being chosen ahead of his Caucasian counterpart to succeed the outgoing editor? The answer, for anyone with a reasonable knowledge of the church, would be clear: *Not a chance in the world!*

Yet that's exactly what happened at Annual Council—in the reverse, of course.

Objectively, it raises disturbing questions. Is fairness important? Does justice matter? What's the role of integrity in the church?

Knowing what I do, I've struggled to fight back cynicism. That has not been easy, when one assesses the pious things people say or write against what, from experience, one knows they are. We get away with it (and we know we will) because 99% of those reading or listening to us are totally in the dark about our political machinations. But it's a little harder for those who've seen a little of the underbelly of the church.

As one who loves the church and wants to do everything to enhance and uphold its good name, it concerns me when things like that happen inside our ranks. Credibility is not a value to be taken lightly in these cynical times. All too often, *what we are shouts so loud people can't hear what we're saying.* This generation, immersed as it is in a sea of hucksterism, can spot fake a mile away. And it should concern us how we are perceived outside the echo chamber of our own offices and deferential committees. Without realizing it, we can come across to outside observers as shysters, not to be taken seriously.

One of the surest ways to develop credibility (whether people agree with us or not) is to do the right thing, the fair thing, the just thing. When Messiah comes, declared the ancient prophet, he will make decisions in "justice," "righteousness will be his belt and faithfulness the sash around his waist" (Isa. 11:4, 5).

As a church, we can talk about revival and reformation all we want, but it could be that God's focus is on the real-life issues that frame the essential conditions of revival. The Old Testament is clear that the Lord is not deceived by our ostentatious expressions of piety. He is not impressed by our pretentious offerings of "thousands of rams," or of "ten thousand rivers of oil." No, what he requires is that (among other things) we "act justly" (Micah 6:6-8), that we "let justice run down like a river, and righteousness like a mighty stream!" (Amos 5:24, NKJV).

That's what God wants.

CHAPTER 16

Worst of Times: My Closing Years at the *Adventist Review*

MY COLLEGE EDUCATION included a class in parliamentary procedure. The idea was to teach students—ministerial students, in particular—how to conduct church and constituency meetings. But one contingent lesson I learned from the experience was that of respect and appropriate deference for the chair or, more broadly, the person legitimately "in charge"—whoever that person happens to be.

So with Bill K's election, I knew as a matter of course that he was to be accorded all the respect and deference befitting the office he'd just acquired. The difficult circumstances surrounding his election notwithstanding, I considered this approach the only professional way to go.

But things did not quite work out that way—which, frankly, was not unexpected. Working in the same office with someone is, in some respects, like a marriage. You get to know them quite well; to size up their personality, their temperament. Yet though I knew Bill and had a pretty good idea what I was in for, I somehow continued to hope, almost against hope, that he'd rise to the occasion and be magnanimous in "victory."

We were off to a good start. About five days after the historic October 8 vote, he stepped into my office just before heading out on a trip to Berrien Springs to attend a meeting of the Biblical Research Institute. I was to call him, if needed. Maybe he'd be glad for the break, he said, laughing. (Often, there's a subtle message buried in these "call me" instructions. Apart from the sense of importance it gives the person being called away, in the eyes of those at the meeting--akin to a physician being paged, that sort of thing--it suggests that the person left in charge is somehow not really "in charge," but must be sure to consult you if any decision of significance needs to be made. Or else, leave themselves open to question if something went wrong—"Why didn't you call?")

"And by the way," he continued, "in connection with our [upcoming] planning day, I'll be doing a memo, perhaps from the airport, on how I want us to proceed, with each staff member leading out on a particular phase of the magazine. I want you to be the first to make a selection as to which phase you will lead."

And my thinking was: *Wow! How generous! I get to choose my assignment first!*

The encounter led to a short journal entry the following day as I reflected on it:

"Again? Roy participating in yet another re-think of the magazines and their operations—for the umpteenth time? For what purpose? My spirit's no longer in it! God, help me! Do I have to do this again? It's exceedingly difficult to see how I can go on."

But go on I did, as reactions continued to pour in. Reginald Robinson called from California to empathize; as did Wintley Phipps from Florida; and former *Adventist Review* colleague Myrna Tetz who, during her time at the magazine was brought to tears more than once from being humiliated by a member of staff who will remain nameless at this point. Among the callers was an elderly Canadian woman from British Columbia, then living in Ontario—and who for years had taken an interest in my education and career. She literally wept over the phone as she lamented what she saw as gross injustice.

Eight days following the vote, Don Schneider, of all people, paid a surprise visit. What I'd been through these many months past could

not have been easy, he said, but he wanted me to know he appreciated the way I comported myself. "You've been nothing short of a
gentleman," he said, "and my respect for you has grown and is growing. And I just wanted to come by and tell you that." That's all he said,
and just as suddenly as he'd appeared, he was gone—the kind of visit
that leaves one wondering: *Did that really happen, or was it just my
imagination.*

So what could I say? It was good of him to come. But why only
then? Was it because everything had now been sewed up, set in concrete? It was difficult not to be cynical about a visit like that. After all,
here was a man who for some eight months had been in cahoots with
Paulsen to have Bill K fill the position now coming by to express con-
dolence. Astonishing, isn't it? You have to give it to people like that.
But at least he came.

By the fourth week of October, our staff had met for two planning
meetings with Bill K in the chair. *"It's a matter of considerable discomfort for me to sit in such meetings,"* I wrote in my journal on October
25, *"planning for the future of* Adventist Review *and* Adventist World
*yet again! I led out at the session last Thursday in the Contents area
of our discussion. Did my best, and the atmosphere was good. But
back of my head was the constant longing to be doing something
else. This morning at staff, as we continued in the planning mode, I
bowed my head, and those around me would have thought I was paying rapt attention to the document in front of me; but I was actually
asking God to get me out of there. How can I function under these
circumstances? Who really cares about what I'm going through at this
difficult time? Who really even knows?"*

As I hinted earlier, during the period leading up to the Annual
Council vote, as well as in the months following, I considered several
options: an opening at the (Columbia Union) *Visitor*; a communication position at the Southern Union; a vice-presidential position at
the Florida Conference; the editorship of *Message* magazine. Nothing
panned out—for economic or logistical reasons, among others. In
respect to the editorship of *Message*, for example (a possibility that

arose in May of 2007), it would have involved, apart from difficult logistical issues, a considerable cut in salary for someone with my years of service.

So I was stuck.

I said above that both Paulsen and Johnsson had used the expression "stoic" to describe my reaction to the developments that were taking place. In a sense, they were correct; but no one knows better than I that I'm still human. I sense things; I feel hurt. And the recent wound was to experience a little scraping at a special meeting not long after Annual Council. Here's how it happened.

Every year, in connection with the North American Division year-end meetings (usually held in the GC complex a few weeks after the end of Annual Council), the *Adventist Review* staff would host a luncheon for all union, conference, and college/university presidents in attendance. It gave us a chance to tout our plans and solicit the support of these leaders. As tends to happen in every office, I coordinated the function one year, and thereafter found the responsibility falling into my lap each time.

And thus it was that about five days after the Annual Council's editorship vote, I commenced preparation for the function. (Bill J had again asked me, several weeks earlier, to plan and coordinate the program.)

The luncheon that year took place October 27; and however awkwardly, I again emceed the event. Roscoe Howard gave a brilliant tribute to Bill J—a classic, really; which was followed by tributes from many of the leaders in attendance. In a 10-minute response, Johnsson recounted highlights of his tenure, eventually coming to recent developments. That very week, he said, Bill K had brought to his attention that in the whole history of the *Review*, there had been only 10 editors. Every editor, Bill K told him, "had first served as an associate, being mentored by the chief editor."

Incidentally, there's always a tendency to sanitize history, so to speak; to anchor it within well-defined contours. But when one actually looks at the evidence, it almost never turns out to be as neat as described—and I'm thinking here both about what Paulsen had said to me in respect to the long-running terms of AR editors and what Johnsson was now repeating from Bill K. Here's how the Adventist encyclopedia summarizes the historical situation vis-à-vis the editors of the magazine:

"Beginning with the first issue [of the paper that eventually became *Adventist Review*], November, 1850, the list reads: 'Publishing Committee' (including James White), 1850-1851; James White, 1851-1855; Uriah Smith, 1855-1861; James White, 1861-1864; Uriah Smith, 1864-1869; J. N. Andrews, 1869-1870; Uriah Smith, 1870-1871; James White, 1871-1872; Uriah Smith, 1872-1873; James White, 1873-1877; Uriah Smith, 1877-1880; James White, 1880-1881 (died Aug. 6, 1881); Uriah Smith, 1881-1897; A. T. Jones, 1897-1901; Uriah Smith, 1901-1903 (died March 6, 1903); W. W. Prescott, 1903-1909; W. A. Spicer, 1909-1911; F. M. Wilcox, 1911-1944; W. A. Spicer 1945 (six months); F. D. Nichol, 1945-[1966]" [*Seventh-day Adventist Encyclopedia* (Washington, D.C.: Review and Herald Publishing Association, 1966, p. 1078, sv. "Review and Herald")].

What we find here is that until F. M. Wilcox, who served for some 33 years, only Uriah Smith had served longer than six years at any one time (16 years, from 1881-1897). In addition, White and Smith, in a veritable musical-chairs scenario, served multiple times, sometimes for as little as one or two years. Clearly, the actual situation was anything but tidy. It wasn't as if one long-serving editor was followed monarchically by another long-serving editor. But it was true that the long-serving Wilcox was followed by three other long-serving editors: F. D. Nichol (21 years), Kenneth Wood (16 years), and William Johnsson (about 24 years).

Continuing his remarks at that year-end function, Johnsson came to what he considered an interesting historical tidbit, also based on what Knott had told him earlier that week: "F. D. Nichol came to the editorship at 48, Kenneth Wood at 48, I at 48, and now Bill Knott at 49. So the age is just right."

Given the fact that Paulsen, until warned of its legal peril, had distinctly brought up the matter of age against me, it seemed insensitive on Johnsson's part to have gone there—and so gratuitously. It was a painful and awkward moment for me, rubbing the sore, as it were. But the Lord helped me through it.

Notwithstanding my intense desire to leave the *Review* during this time, all options seem closed. It was one of the most discouraging periods of my entire ministry. *"It is at once humbling and humiliating,"* I wrote in my journal in the period immediately following. *"I'm trying to avoid losing faith in everyone and everything. My hope is in God alone. I continue to believe He'll yet bring me through this. He will lift my head. He knows the way that I take; and when He has tried me, I will come forth as gold. I believe God sees my discouragement, and He understands. And I'm not discouraged that Bill K got the job. I'm discouraged and dispirited that I'm so utterly stuck in my position, seemingly with no way out! O God, how I want out of here!"*

But I thank God for the resiliency of the human spirit, for the ability He gives us to pick up the pieces and move on. The Sabbath following that year-end luncheon just described, I taught my Sabbath School class, then in the afternoon made a journal entry that now reminds me of how I began to transition from the intense feelings of wanting to vacate my job at *Adventist Review* to settling down to the status quo. The entry went as follows:

"This afternoon I'm feeling surprisingly at peace. It's as if I'm getting reconciled to my situation and seeing how I can cope within it. The explorations I've made thus far [with several employing entities] have not worked out; no prospects developed that matched my interest or skills. So I guess this Sabbath afternoon, as I said to my wife last night as we talked, I'm thinking that, bad as the situation is for me, I still have a job. And if worse comes to worst, I can make the best of it. I'm deciding not to sell myself cheap, either at my present job or at some new opening. I don't want to act precipitously and regret later. I remain ready to move if something suitable turns up; but as of this minute, I've stopped searching. I must batten down now, and see how to make the best of my present situation."

My journal entry for 10/31/06 was a kind of follow up to that Sabbath afternoon resolution; and as I came back to it in preparing these materials, I was surprised by its cold realism. It read, as follows:

"I've learned so much through this experience. No one really stays awake about your situation. People move on. And what you have to do is move on as well. Accept no one's pity. Chin up! Just carry on to the very best of your ability. Don't cower to anyone. Don't be afraid of anyone. Don't carry around a grudge for anyone. Don't be tom-fooled by anyone. Don't be impressed by the pretended piousness of anyone. Don't be taken in by empty words about diversity and unity and 'listening to one another' and all that kind of garbage. Take a look first at who is saying these words, and how the words comport with their personal track record."

It was a cold but realistic appraisal of the path ahead for me.

Behind the Scenes in the Office

Bright and early on January 2, the first working day of 2007, Paulsen unexpectedly dropped by my office. "We have not talked since annual council," he said, "and we should have." He wanted to let me know that he had confidence in my work and wanted me to stay at the *Review.* He didn't want me to interpret my not being chosen editor as in any way suggesting displeasure with my work. So he was urging me to stay. It was a tense but reasonably pleasant meeting, though he left with no indication on my part as to what I might do or not do. I got the impression that he had had nightmares about my leaving the *Review,* thus confronting him with the task of finding two associates at the same time—one to replace Bill K, and the other to replace me. I did a lot of listening during our conversation, without saying much of substance.

As the weeks of the New Year rolled on, life in the office settled into its usual hectic routine, with its numerous demands and deadlines. Everyone—I especially—was conscious of operating under new management and in uncharted waters. And given the unpredictability of the new captain, the question back of my head was: *When will the clampdown begin?*

For me the first sign came around the third week of the New Year, three weeks after Knott had taken the reins. It was over an editorial I'd written for *Adventist Review* to coincide with the 2007 Black History Month. Entitled "The Pictures on Our Walls," the piece zeroed in on the racial disparity that has characterized the topmost administrative positions in the Adventist Church over its history, indirectly epitomizing everything that had transpired in the recent past, precisely in regard to the AR editorship struggle. (If you visit the General Conference [GC] building today, you will notice that editors in chief of the *Adventist Review* are among the top church leaders who get their pictures posted on the wall somewhere within or near their departments—portraits reaching back to the earliest occupants of the office.)

About two weeks into our five-week production cycle, Bill sent me a note, taking issue with the piece. Before sharing his objections, perhaps it would be helpful to refresh readers on what I'd written. So here (in italics) is the full text of the editorial in question:

In January this year, former Seinfeld star Michael Richards shocked Americans when his stand-up comedy routine went berserk. Heckled by two Blacks in the audience, Richards let fly a barrage of insulting profanities laced with what's known in the U.S. as the "n" word. The customary apologies followed. And as Richards stood contrite by the side of Jesse Jackson for one of these, it was hard to believe that that was the same guy who'd uttered such foul obscenities against Jackson's fellow Blacks less than 40 hours earlier.

Which begs the question: What are people really like in their true selves, behind closed doors, away from the cameras and microphones? The heckling blew the lid off something in Richards, but nothing could have emerged that hadn't been there before.

This is Black History Month in the United States, a time when members of the Black community try to bring to the attention of the larger population the contributions of Black Americans to the history and life of our country. If an observer from outside the Adventist Church were to examine our speeches and our public statements, they'd say: "These people don't need any such reminders!" Would they be right?

One of the best things the Adventist Church has going for it in this respect is the life and example of Ellen G. White. Her statements on slavery in the U.S., her concern for "the southern work" in her time, and her general counsels on race have served as a huge source of ethnic stability in the church. "The religion of the Bible recognizes no caste or color," she said. "It ignores rank, wealth, worldly honor. God estimates men as men. With Him, character decides their worth" (Testimonies for the Church, vol. 9, p. 223).

But our track record has not been great. And the scary thing is that if such vitriol could reside in as funny and likable a guy as Michael Richards, who knows what demons lurk in the rest of us! We don't. What seems evident among us, however, is a deep-seated, more respectable reality, that over the years has kept certain people in their place.

Imagine a Black youngster approaching their Adventist-worker parents with these questions: "Dad/Mom, are all positions in the church open, or are some closed to people like me? Are there glass ceilings in the church?" What would be the honest answer from an informed Adventist parent?

In George Orwell's brilliant political satire Animal Farm, the animals come up with seven commandments, the last of which proclaimed "all animals . . . equal." But as some of the four-legged creatures drifted closer and closer to adopting the ways of the humans they'd overthrown, one group among them secretly added a rider to the seventh injunction to make it read: "All animals are equal, but some animals are more equal than others." Is that a reality in our church?

We've been in existence now for more than 160 years; and we've represented ourselves as an interracial, multicultural, multiethnic global community. But what do our actions say?

That thought came to me about three or four years ago as I walked the halls of the GC, looking at the pictures that adorn the walls of key

departments in the building—pictures of the church's topmost offi-
cials over the years. I counted 92 leaders, 89 of them (96.7 percent)
Caucasian. This one reality trumps all our professions about diversity.
They tell the story of a glass ceiling beyond which certain folks cannot
rise. It's as if there's an unwritten understanding that certain positions
in the church are too sensitive for certain ethnic groups to occupy.
The United Nations can afford to take that risk, but the church is
much too delicate for that!

Multitudes of those affected will never notice. But the number
of those paying attention is rising, and it hurts the church. People
tune out. They become jaded, cynical. They see through our studied
speeches, our proper, well-chosen words.

But the ultimate tragedy would be to surrender to cynicism. The
better approach is to look beyond walls and ceilings to the One who
stands above it all, and who has no respect for persons. Keeping ever
in mind the splendid vision held out before us—the vision of "a great
multitude . . . from every nation, tribe, people and language . . . before
the throne [of God]" (Rev. 7:9).

At the end of the day, isn't that what it's all about?

That's what I'd written. And now for Bill's objections:

"I've been thinking this past week about the editorial you [recent-
ly] placed [in production]...," Bill wrote to me in an email memo,
dated Sunday afternoon, January 21, 2007. "As usual, the piece is
well-crafted, earnest, and makes an important point.

"I'm wondering, however, if the net effect of the editorial might
not be unintentionally misleading as regards the current situation of
top leadership at the GC. You refer to seeing the many pictures of
leaders on the wall who served in the church's past, 96.7 % of whom
were Caucasian as you noted it, but don't refer to the current diversity evident among top GC officers and departmental leaders. As far
as I know, among 3 top officers and 13 department heads, there are
4 persons of African descent; 4 of Asian or Pacific Island descent;
and 8 Caucasians. The current situation represents the efforts of the

world church to correct the historic imbalance of which you accurately wrote.

"I want to both support the excellent point you've made about diversity and encourage as accurate a portrayal of the current situation as possible.

"If you'd like to talk briefly about this tomorrow, I'd be pleased to take the time."

The same day I responded, as follows:

"Hi Bill:

"I tried to write the editorial in question (as I do all others) as carefully as I can. The points you made in your note are well taken, but they don't directly relate to the issue of the piece. The key here is in the title; and the point it wants to make, in the context of Black History Month, is that with all our diversity, the topmost positions of the church (those that merit the posting of the photos in question) seem, to a large degree, closed to certain minorities, as evidenced from more than 160 years of Adventist history. If that point was not made clear enough, I'm sure I can make it even more explicit at [the] dummy [stage of production].

"Let me know if you have any further questions."

We didn't talk more about the matter, and the editorial ran as written. I suspect that either the logic of the piece was too strong to shake, or Bill's sea legs at that point were still too weak and unsteady for him to put his foot down. But I was under no illusions. I knew that he'd certainly make clear in future encounters who was in charge.

(If you get the impression in what follows that there were constant battles in the office, then that would be wrong. Bill can be very charming, and things in the office could at times be very pleasant. Besides, professionalism continued to be the name of the game for me, and constant conflict is not part of my DNA. Office politics, with its never-ending squabbles and skirmishes, weary me. And months would go by without a ruffle. But there was another side of Bill, a side that outsiders would never see—a side exposed, however, to those who work up close. Hence the points of conflict described below.)

The weeks rolled by following the scuffle about the editorial. And just about two months later, as I arrived at work Monday morning, March 26, I found a memo from Bill on my chair (which, I suspected, all other staffers received). It dealt with work and vacation regulations. It frowned on the idea of AR staff working off-site and generally sought to tighten up on working hours and vacation time—for both salaried and hourly personnel.

What I knew quite well from my years at *Adventist Review* was that we have a hard-working bunch of people at that office. I couldn't remember anyone on staff who didn't *regularly* take work home. With the frequent meetings, constant telephone calls, and other interruptions during a typical work day, it was sometimes difficult to complete all one's editing and writing assignments during regular office hours. So you took stuff home, sometimes working late into the night, and hurrying back to the office the following morning to attend meetings or track other deadlines. It was not unusual for that to happen several times a month. (Ask our spouses, and they will tell you that it was as if some of us were married to our work.) Each of us had a weekly deadline to meet. It wasn't something you could bluff around or cover over with padding. If your stuff wasn't ready it showed at (what we called in our internal office lingo) *folder time*—the deadline moment for articles to be submitted for a particular issue.

That being the case at the office, Bill's memo came as a big surprise—an insult, in fact; and later in the day I went to talk to him about it.

It was not a pleasant encounter. He argued he'd "waited 90 days" before issuing the memo; that he had vetted it with several (unnamed) entities and people in the building (including HR). And that that is what would normally be expected according to policy. (I couldn't remember ever hearing Bill J use the word "policy" in that context in 18 years of working with him). He'd noticed numerous violations on our staff, he said—people taking off early, and absenting themselves without prior notice. He was surprised the previous Friday to come into the office and discover that both Steve Chavez and I had been absent. (And hearing that, I thought to myself: *Can he really be refer-ring to Steve, a veritable workhorse for the magazine, the one who puts in such long hours and days tracking some of the most compli-cated and tedious aspects of our production process? Bill has the gall to cite this dedicated worker for being gone on a Friday morning after he'd slaved his way through the rest of the week!?*)

He'd noticed, he continued, that I'd been gone the past three Fridays; and when that happens, it increases the volume of traffic for him. (Incidentally, we would hardly have any traffic volume to speak of on the typical Friday morning—with the office closing at noon. Besides, many—if not most—of the other departments in the com-plex were virtually closed on Fridays; and our own deadline for each week was Thursday. A smattering of items from time to time would land on a senior editor's desk on a Friday morning, and that we could anticipate after reading the folder Thursday. If we were in the office, we handled it Friday, of course. But in most cases such items could well wait to be processed the following Monday, which would still be two or more weeks earlier than the time the chief editor typically had his own materials ready. And the astonishing thing is that as he spoke to me, he was well aware that I knew that. After all, one of my duties was to track what items were ready and what weren't every week as I read the folder.)

Going five months back into history, he noted I'd been gone sev-eral days the previous November—which would have been before he officially took office.

My mouth fell open at that last reference, a startling example of office surveillance and elephant memory. (He was referring to a time when, facing a January 2007 deadline for submitting the manuscript of the Sabbath School Quarterly companion book, I'd taken a few days off to work on the document.) When I explained that to him, he responded that projects like that would be out of order if they con-flicted with work at the office. When requested to participate in such endeavors, he said, editors should ask how it would contribute to the work of the office. (For anyone familiar with the scholarly enterprise in the Adventist church, and with the generally accepted unwritten protocols governing writing projects for the church, Bill's statement was a mind-blowing thought! It was the most crippling notion I'd come across during my entire time at the GC. Had such a policy been in place during my previous years at the office, I'd not have been able to write a single book.)

People are getting appointments to their pet places, he said, and is that helping the magazine? People are taking more vacation than what they're entitled to; etc., etc.

A very good debater, Bill handles himself well, and never backs down. NEVER! I couldn't shake him on a single point. (Of course, it helps when you know that because of rank, you always get to have the final word, regardless of the merits of the other guy's position.) I remember asking him at one point in the conversation whether it was a control issue for him. No, he replied, I'm just enforcing policy. "You should have known that a new administration may want to do things differently," he said. Bill J's leadership style was loose and casual, he noted, but his would be different.

These were the opening salvos of what would turn into a series of perfectly unnecessary battles. Like that over staff travel, for example. Now that he was editor, Bill sought to assert tight control on the travel front. A memo from him, dated August 26, 2007, contained, among other things, a primer on how to fill out a travel authorization request form. And you can only imagine how humiliating it was for me to be receiving such a memo. The part that irked the most was the directive that "When submitting a written Travel Authorization form before traveling, [we should] please also attach a brief statement that identifies how this travel will help to achieve the magazines' goals for subscription growth, author recruitment, or representation."

Ever since I arrived at the GC, travel request forms always carried a "purpose of travel" section—requiring a line such as: "To speak for camp meeting," or "for graduation," or "for church anniversary." That was nothing new. What was galling in this new mandate was the thought that a whole paragraph of explanation was now needed. In other words, at my level of seniority I was being required to justify to Bill the need for every trip I make, even before I could say yes to the entity requesting my service.

During Bill J's time, I would put a travel request for signing on his assistant's desk and know that I'd have it back the same day—or the following, if he wasn't around. Sometimes I'd simply take the piece of paper directly to him, and he would sign it. Under the new regime, it was a must that that piece of paper go through his assistant, and I can remember sometimes having to wait as many as ten days or longer to get it back.

(Keep in mind that the travel budgets for traveling GC personnel were voted by GC administration—not by that traveler's individual department. In voting those budgets, the committee took into consideration the particular worker's job description, seniority, and worldwide responsibilities in the mission of the church. And if a person did not have enough common sense and good judgment to plan their travels in such a way as to benefit the organization, as well as their own department, then they really did not belong in that category. Thus I considered it an unnecessary irritant to be required to write a little essay justifying each and every travel appointment I took.)

It all led to another heated discussion with Bill. And—you guessed it—he stood his ground once again, budging not a single millimeter. Deeply peeved, I went to Paulsen a couple of weeks later (September 11) to lodge a formal complaint. I was dealing with an authoritarian situation, I told him, that had practically reduced me to the level of an assistant editor, if not lower. I expressed my intention to retire, unless I could be reassigned.

In retrospect, it was a precipitous and ill-advised move on my part, and it led to no good result that I can remember. In the first place, Paulsen had nothing to offer as an alternative (and I was sure he'd not be sitting up nights worrying about reassigning me, especially when my leaving the magazine would plunge him into the double trouble of finding two associates, instead of just one to replace Bill); and in the second place, as I would discover, I really was not ready for retirement—either psychologically or in regard to years of service.

Still, foolhardily, I proceeded to draw up a memorandum of understanding, outlining to Bill K a list of conditions under which I'd agree to remain at the *Review*. If Bill was OK with these conditions, then I would not send a formal letter to Paulsen requesting reassignment, as Paulsen had requested.

For the life of me, I cannot now remember if I ever actually sent the memorandum; but the draft document, as it appears in my journal, clearly indicates the deep frustration I was experiencing at the time. Here are four of the seven conditions I outlined (and the segments in round and square parentheses also formed part of the original document as I drew it up):

1. "That I would be left free to manage my travel and appointments schedule, in the same (responsible) way I've been doing it for the past 18 years. [[During this entire period, there's been no crisis or any abnormal hardship or embarrassment in regard to the operation of the office....]]

2. That I be left free to manage my time in and out of the office, without oversight or suspicion. [I think I'm familiar with the needs of the office and do not absent myself helter skelter. In fact, over the years, few other staff have spent longer hours at their desk. But there are times when the kind of work I'm doing at the moment demands quiet, protracted, uninterrupted time. I want to feel free to manage that, without having to be second-guessed. After all, we have no furloughs in this job, and no one should begrudge the measly day we take here and there for close study and creative work—especially when care is taken to ensure those times do not conflict with urgent production assignments.]

3. That I would not be required to justify my out-of-town appointments and travels. [What I mean here is that I should be treated with the dignity and respect my seniority deserves. I want it understood without my having to explain it for each

appointment that I'm always aware that I'm traveling for the church and the magazines. It serves no essential purpose for me to legalistically write this out for every appointment I take]

4. That I would be consulted on the ground floor in regard to major initiatives coming up for decision, and not have to hear them at the same time with the rest of the staff."

Whether or not I ever sent this memorandum, I did communicate with Bill on all the elements it contained. But there was absolutely no budge on his part. He was completely tone deaf to the plea that lay behind all my approaches on these issues—a plea for respect, given my seniority; a plea to not be held to juvenile, legalistic requirements after more than 18 years on the job. All I needed to hear from him was some sentence like "Roy, don't sweat it. I trust you to do the right thing." Instead, he doubled down each time, reiterating to me past directives he'd sent out, and emphasizing that it all applied to me "as well as the rest of the staff."

In other words, just suck it up.

Such conflicts never would have arisen if Bill had taken me into his confidence—I at that point being the only associate. When he was editor, Bill J frequently would call in his two associates (Bill K and me) for consultation on a variety of problems, issues, and upcoming plans and initiatives. So that when major items got to staff, his two associates had already been briefed. Things drastically changed under the new management. Now I was getting information the same time as the rest of the staff—usually through memos or announcements in staff meetings. I was out of the loop in regard to new initiatives or changes—both minor and major. At one point in my journal I recorded that I'd not been involved in any consultation or planning at the senior editors' level "in nine months." Bill simply ran the show all by himself.

Even in areas involving my own specific responsibilities, I sometimes was left to discover things purely by accident. On 10/4/07, I journaled, as follows:

"It's the second time in as many weeks that I've been blindsided by Bill. The first came two Fridays ago when [marketing director] Claude [Richli] called out to me from his office as I was passing by: 'Roy, would you mind if I take over the approval of ads for the magazine?' 'It's a job I'd been wanting to unload for a long while,' I called back to him, turning around and approaching his office, 'so I really wouldn't mind. But we've always considered it an editorial function, and not something that belongs to marketing. But you may want to bring this up with Bill, and we can—the three of us—discuss the matter together.'

Suddenly, I felt impressed to ask him: 'Have you and Bill talked about this?' 'Yes,' he said. 'And he's given you the go-ahead on that?' 'Yes, he has.' And that's when I hit the ceiling. 'Bill gave you the go-ahead without any consultation with me?' Which led him to back off, feeling that he'd probably said more than he should.

As we talked some more, he indicated to me that, as he understood it, ad approval was part of his job description as assistant publisher."

And that's when I learned for the first time that he was also assistant publisher. Bill had briefed me on his intention to recommend his name as marketing director, but had mentioned nothing about assistant publisher. And I must have been traveling and, therefore, absent from the board meeting that voted the particular office. The minutes of that meeting had clearly not been shared with me, nor had any memo circulated in the office on the subject. So I'd been completely in the dark. And the whole episode left me feeling diminished.

My journal also noted a second incident of this kind:

"This morning [my administrative assistant] mentioned to me that Bill K had asked her to divide her time into three parts—one part for me, one for Claude Richli, and one for her other duties. She was talking to me about that, she said, because she noticed that I'd not said anything to her about it, and suspected I'd not been informed. And she was correct."

I tried to put the best face I could on the awkward matter, saying as little to her, as possible. But, of course, I instantly saw the development as a violation of fundamental office protocol and elementary courtesy. I mean, even if a CEO intends to act without consultation, they should, at the very least, inform all affected parties, don't you think? It's Administration 101!

I was to encounter numerous other incidents of this kind; and was often embarrassed when staff members would come to me for explanations and clarifications of this or that plan or initiative, thinking that I'd been part of the decision-making.

It all contributed to a growing desire to leave the magazine, with retirement looking more and more as the only viable option left. But the economic situation in the country at the time was a reality I had to face. I also had to take into consideration that my service record fell a few years short of the place where I wanted it to be. Yet, although I was confused about exactly what to do, it did seem clear to me that I'd done my time at the *Review*. Besides, another issue loomed large before me. Based on past experience, I saw the upcoming GC session (for which we at the magazine would begin preparing months and months in advance) as a period filled with strenuous work and tension-producing elements. And I prayed to the Lord often for release before that time came.

Eventually, it became a matter of survival—day to day, week to week, month to month. God helping me, I summoned the strength to settle into the status quo, taking every day as it came. In the sentiments of a statement I heard somewhere, I had to discipline myself against excessive frustration and anger, summoning all the internal resources I had, aided by divine power. There is a resiliency of the human spirit, especially when empowered by the Divine Spirit.

CHAPTER 17

Retirement Saga—a Tale of Frustration, Embarrassment, and Relief

FOR AN ADVENTIST worker, the decision to retire does not come easy. And it did not for me. In fact, it turned out to be a very complicated affair; and in some respects (because of my own miscalculations), both humiliating and embarrassing.

After missing the first deadline I'd given myself for submitting my retirement letter to Paulsen, I sat down in my study Sabbath afternoon, June 6, 2009, reflecting on my intention to finally do it Monday, June 8. Over the last days of May and early June, the retirement decision that had been solidifying in my mind for months was enhanced by a minor, unexpected development in the office.

As chair of our scheduling committee, I'd sent out a notice that for its next meeting—given a conflict we were at the time facing in the office—the group should convene on a Tuesday afternoon, instead of Wednesday, our usual meeting time. In response to that memo, fellow-associate editor Gerald Klingbeil (who had recently joined the staff) sent me a reply that surprised me. Requesting that the meeting be held Tuesday morning instead, he gave this explanation: "Tuesday is usually my research day, but in view of the extraordinary [situation] I would be happy to come in on Tuesday morning."

A "research day"! *What a wonderful idea!* I thought. Our

colleagues on college and university campuses get three to six months of furlough from time to time, but editors of the church's flagship paper, writing for the entire denomination, receive no time off. They're expected to come up with fresh, insightful ideas every week, while keeping their noses perpetually to the grind. It hardly makes sense.

So my first reaction was: *Good for him! A research day!*

But then I began to reflect some more. Why, as an associate editor, did I have to learn about that special arrangement in this indirect way? Would it not have been the courteous thing to have received a formal briefing on that detail? And as my mind continued to exercise on the issue, the thought struck me: *Here I was, doing double duty all during Bill K's study leave—with no thanks for it; and here I was, picking up the added work during the long search for a new associate (lasting about two and a half years!) after Bill was elected editor; and here I was, still picking up additional stuff every Tuesday, while the new associate is given one day a week off for research!*

There had to be something wrong with that picture. And it made me more determined than ever to bring an end to my stay at the magazine. "So, God willing," I said to myself, "it's Monday! I will turn in my retirement notice Monday."

And that I did.

Then getting back to my office, I wrote in my journal, as follows:

"June 8, 2009—Monday, 7:35 a.m. The die has been cast! The retirement notices have been delivered—first to Paulsen (left on his assistant's desk), then to Bill (left on his desk). It was eerie walking up to Paulsen's office—not for a meeting, but to deliver a retirement letter. The hallways were dark—folks had not yet arrived. The normally motion-sensitive lights in his administrative assistant's office did not switch on as I entered. The traffic on Route 29 [that runs by the GC building] was light as I walked back down the stairwell; I watched my reflection in the glass, trying to figure out my mood. I knew it was something I'd have to do sometime, yet having done it, I feel a sense of apprehension, for some reason. Now I await the response and reaction."

RETIREMENT SAGA—A TALE OF FRUSTRATION, EMBARRASSMENT, AND RELIEF▶

"June 11, 2009. The past couple of days since the announcement have been strange. Spirits low, in realization of the enormity of the decision. [My oldest sister] Maudlyn's reaction was: 'Better to walk out than be carried out.' [My sister] Flossie's reaction, like that of [my daughter] Kim was: 'Why? Why now?' Then, deep down, there is a subtle second-guessing on my part."

When Paulsen responded on June 12, four days later, he began by explaining he'd been gone an entire month from the office (to Kazakhstan, China, etc.)—small talk. Then getting to my retirement letter, he expressed respect for my decision, and mentioned he'd been told that I was the longest serving associate editor in the history of the *Review*. (I'm sure the irony of this did not dawn on him). He recalled we'd talked about the matter of retirement about a year earlier, but that, in regard to reassignment, nothing had turned up that he felt would be fit for me, or provide the kind of challenge my training would deserve. Even now as we spoke, he said, there is nothing he could offer. "So I guess it is what it is," he said. He expressed appreciation for my work over the years, commending me for keeping a balance, not going too far either side of the road. (Really?) It was a brief conversation—lasting only about four minutes.

It didn't take long for the enormity of the retirement decision to bear down on me, and the ensuing developments would lead to some of the most humiliating and embarrassing moments of this entire episode—perhaps even my entire ministry.

The Sabbath following that last conversation with Paulsen found Celia and me in Atlanta, Georgia, spending time at our son's place. That afternoon, after working on sermons for an upcoming Alberta (Canada) appointment, I found myself unable to sleep when I lay down beside my wife, already resting. Suddenly, all the implications of retirement came crashing down on me, chiefly centered around financial considerations, intruding themselves upon the holy Sabbath.

Should I call Paulsen and inform him that I'd given the matter further consideration and had decided to stay on a little longer? But how would that go over?

I struggled with myself. To give your formal word and then go back on it? I went back and forth in my mind on the issue, waiting for my wife to wake up. At one point I wished I'd been the one asleep—and dreaming—and that I'd wake up to find that I'd not actually submitted a retirement notice, after all. I struggled, too, with the strange notion of becoming a non-person, as it were, following retirement.

Going through such psychological turmoil was the last thing I'd expected. It shook me up.

Finally, my wife awoke, and when I told her about it, she immediately thought I'd been affected by what others had said—one of my sisters and my daughter, in particular. She might have been correct, but I got the impression that these thoughts had been operating in the background of my mind all along, independent of any external input. She discounted the economic considerations and calculations I'd made, and fully thought we could manage. It would not be a good idea to go back on your word, she said, reminding me that people usually go through these psychological, second-guessing moments in the wake of major decisions.

I agreed, and decided to stick to my decision.

But by Monday morning (June 15) the feelings returned. I was sensing an emptiness I couldn't understand—something akin to what others would describe as depression. I felt as if I'd virtually become nothing, absolutely unimportant, a nonentity, if you know what I mean. I had these sermons to prepare, and it was as if I had no energy for them. I felt spent. Perhaps some of you reading these lines can relate. It was sheer mental turmoil.

That morning I wrote in my journal:

"No one knows how I'm feeling now. When I open my mouth, the words and voice sound the same. My granddaughter is in the house, and she's a bag of fun. I'm smiling, giggling, laughing, teasing, but I feel an emptiness inside, a lost-ness, a disconnection. It's as if I'm going berserk; and yet I'm completely calm on the outside. I never expected to feel this way. Did I retire for the wrong reasons? All of a sudden, the work I dreaded at the [upcoming] GC session seems minimal in

comparison with what I'm going through now. I feel as if I'd welcome all that work now. I even looked at my incoming emails, perchance there'd be some last-minute appeal for me to stay on. Nothing. Yet I must go on; I cannot afford to show weakness now."

Hat in Hand

For those not familiar with the phrase "hat in hand," it means, according to the dictionary, to approach a situation or another person "in an attitude of respectful humility," as in the expression: "He had to go *hat in hand* to apologize."

Something like that is what developed at this point in my retirement saga, and I wrote the following in my journal:

"The announcement [that I was retiring] was made at the Adventist Review *board meeting on June 16. (I did not attend, even though I was then back in Washington.) The next day I sat down with GC secretary Matthew Bediako to brief him on that notice and on other developments. He expressed surprise that I did not wait until the GC session, slated for June-July of the following year, explaining the special financial benefits (tantamount to five months of severance pay) for leaders who are voted out of office at the session—to tide them over while they searched for other employment. And that same arrangement, he said, would apply to all senior GC personnel retiring at or just after the session."*

This was critical information for me. To not go for such a benefit would be foolhardy on my part, after working all these years for the church.

I left his office in crisis mode, going home to a restless night (June 17), and awaking about 4:45, unable to go back to sleep. Later, I described my reaction in my journal:

"The new situation is hitting me harder than ever. Something about retirement isn't sitting well with me. It's as if I'm entering a realm of non-existence. I keep wishing I am dreaming and will wake up. But, unfortunately, I am awake. I can't see Celia not attending the GC session 'in style,' as it were. I want her to attend one more time

in a privileged position [as the spouse of a delegate]. *However crass, those are my thoughts. And for myself, I can't picture staying at* [our son's] *house* [the session was to be in Atlanta] *and having to commute to the venue from there. It all appears monumentally awkward to me. And all of a sudden, struggling with the bulletins* [before, at, and after the session] *begins to look more and more attractive in comparison."*

It was a time for earnest, fervent prayer. I was in crisis. And the only one who knew it. Leaning heavily on the strong promise of Psalm 20:1, 2, I wondered how God would get me through this predicament of my own making. Later I would record what developed:

"The idea that came to me was to call Paulsen. I asked the Lord to impress me otherwise if He thought I shouldn't go back on my word. About 8:30, June 18, I placed the call. [On the eve of my trip to Alberta, I was working from home that day]. *He was not in the office, but his assistant had him call me shortly thereafter. 'I'm speaking to you,' I said to him when he called, 'as one pastor to another. Something you said in our conversation last Friday* [when he'd called after receiving my retirement letter] *has kept reverberating in my mind ever since. You probably didn't even hear it—it was very gentle. You weren't pressing. But your words were: "But Roy, if you change your mind, we'd be delighted." Well, I'm calling to say that I'm leaning toward postponing the date by a year, if it's not too late.'"*

Groveling, that's what it was—plain and simple. Groveling. Hat in hand, tail between my legs. I'm embarrassed to tell it, but that's what happened. Paulsen's response was immediate: "Certainly," he said, "it's not too late, Roy. Not at all." He then went on to express his relief, given the upcoming GC session. We talked about how Bill and the rest of the staff would be informed. And so the call ended.

Contrary to the regular pattern I'd followed until then, I'd not talked to Celia before calling Paulsen. The matter was so delicate and personal that I felt no one else on earth—not even my wife—could possibly understand the psychological turmoil I was passing through. I had to act. And I had to act alone.

When I called her at work to brief her on what I'd done, she was devastated. She felt hurt that I didn't consult her first. And she was correct. I admitted it and apologized. But I'd been almost beside my-self, and I feared she might have discouraged me from proceeding. It was a most awkward situation. She felt betrayed and terribly humili-ated. It was a tough time for me. As uncomfortable as it gets!

"Yet," I journaled on June 30, 12 days later, "I felt an inner peace that I'd done what I needed to, however difficult and humiliating for me. I needed the extra time for many reasons, perhaps chiefly psycho-logical and economic."

And so it was that I continued at my post, with what I interpreted as genuine relief on the part of the entire staff, including Bill. The usual frantic pace continued, with the staff beginning to shift into pre-GC-session mode shortly after the beginning of the New Year. Once again, I was in charge of coordinating the bulletins for the session, a complicated and protracted process, involving numerous commu-nications with all 13 world divisions, plus the heads of GC depart-ments, services, and institutions. Reports from all of these entities had to be requested, received, edited, then re-edited for length; hundreds of photos had to be processed, with all captions checked and double-checked for accuracy and relevance; delinquent entities had to be contacted again and again, with follow-up emails and letters; and on and on. Exhausting stuff!

I would have resented doing all this yet again, except for the re-cent developments that had brought me to it. In a sense, I'd asked for it. And once again, I threw all my energies into the task. At the session itself, apart from finding space for the numerous stories generated on site, one also had to make room for those (solicited) reports from divisions, departments, services and institutions of the church, while tracking all the proceedings and actions of the session as they came to us from GC secretariat. In addition, we had to make sure that all ads (paid for in advance) found places in the bulletins.

It is a nerve-racking, daily grind, and one for which the entire editorial and production teams came together in the same big room— the entire *Adventist Review* editorial and support staff, as well as key members of the production team from the Review and Herald Publishing Association. As the multitude of documents made their way from one hand to another, one desk to another, one computer to another, everyone had a single goal in mind—to accomplish in one day what ordinarily would spread across five weeks or so.

The end of each day—anytime between 5 and 7 p.m.—was a time of relief, as we looked back on one more day's assignment done. The edited materials, flowed into our computer system on the ground, had now been transmitted electronically to the Review and Herald in Hagerstown, Maryland, where those production staff members who'd stayed behind labored through the night to print, ship, and get the next day's bulletins to the floor of the session by 9:00 a.m.

The quinquennial GC sessions have become a virtual Adventist Mecca, an event most members would like to experience at least once. The coming together of God's people from all across the planet and from all cultures of the earth is something to behold. The preaching, the music, the singing, and (perhaps the most treasured of all) the fellowship. Friends and acquaintances who'd not seen one another in years or even decades meet at a session. It's a sea of handshakes, hugs, and kisses. Everywhere!

And staying at my post just a little longer gave me one more opportunity to share in this glorious experience one more time in an official capacity. But however much I enjoyed it, I knew it was going to be the last time I would attend as a member of the *Adventist Review* delegation, so to speak. Not long after the session, in a letter dated July 28, 2010, I (again) gave formal notice of my intention to retire around the time of that year's annual council, with the specific effective date left open. But this time the notification would go to a different president.

The election of the president is usually one of the first items of business as a GC session convenes, preceded only by the organizing of the nominating committee, itself preceded by the report of the current president. It's a report that—to be perfectly crass about it—constitutes a campaign speech of sorts, saying, in effect, to the assembly:

"Look at what has been accomplished during my term! And don't you think I deserve another one?"

In a sense, the delegates expect that. But there are moments when there's also an expectation of change, when attendees hope that a sitting president, having taken due credit for the accomplishments of his term (or terms), would graciously throw in the towel, big-heartedly making way for someone else.

And as the 75-year old Paulsen stood to give his report that opening evening in Atlanta, the expectation was that he would do just that, especially given the fact that he'd caused others in the past to be shown the door on account of their age, and also considering the close call he had had at the previous session (in St. Louis), when, I understand, just seven votes separated him from runner-up Ted Wilson. Instead, with all ears in the giant stadium perked as he neared the critical end of his report, he rambled his way through an inelegant statement, whose basic message, nevertheless, was clear: *My hat is still in the ring.*

That was Thursday evening, June 24, 2010. By Sunday, as we worked on the materials for Bulletin # 3, which would carry Paulsen's critical remarks, a new president, Ted Wilson, had been elected. That's when Claude Sabot, an associate in secretariat, dropped by our office, and both he and Bill approached me in my role as bulletin coordinator. Sabot's suggestion, in which Bill concurred (and in which I saw light), was that Paulsen's unsteady remarks at the end of his report would not stand him in good stead and, as a courtesy to him, might better be omitted from the minutes in the bulletin.

I promised to watch out for the item as the production process went forward. But, swamped in a blizzard of reports and papers, the detail slipped my mind, and the remarks were published as delivered. I apologized to Bill for the slipup. I fully had intended to yank the awkward paragraphs from the minutes.

But, in retrospect, it's a slipup I no longer regret. After all, that's what happened. It was a public statement, delivered in front of a world audience. And it deserves to be preserved for posterity. For obvious reasons, it would be inappropriate to reproduce it here; but the curious will know where to find it.

I have no idea if Paulsen ever noticed his own words in the bulletin, let alone if they brought him any embarrassment, as Sabot thought they would. But if they did, and if he ever knew how they got to be left in, it would have marked the second time that I'd have run afoul of him in the bulletins. The first time was in St. Louis in 2005, and what role that incident played in denying me the editorship of *Adventist Review*, I will probably never know.

But it was lunchtime when I happened upon Kari Paulsen, her husband by her side, in the session cafeteria. "Roy," she said abruptly as I approached them, "why did you put that horrible picture of us in the *Review*? It looked like death warmed over." And as she spoke, it was obvious to me that the two had discussed the matter.

Stunned and blindsided, I was at a loss as to how to respond. It had been touted by Bill Johnsson, so she knew I was in charge of the bulletins, and her comments had been well directed. What she did not know, however, was that the entire editorial staff played their separate roles, and were responsible for various functions. Photos like theirs, for example, came under news—which was Bill Knott's domain. When he and his team had made their best photo selections, I would have had neither time nor inclination to second-guess them.

But my presence of mind failed me that day. Though we usually take the blame for one another, it would have been entirely proper in that circumstance to let Mrs. Paulsen know how things came together for the bulletins; and then direct her to Bill K who headed up our news division. I might have said something like: "It is true I'm in charge of the bulletins, but I don't micro-manage the process. We've divided the responsibilities, and our news contingent is responsible for the images we run. Bill K oversees that department, and I will ask him to contact you to explain, perhaps, some of the constraints they were working with as they selected the particular photo."

That would have been entirely proper, but it did not occur to me to say that. So I took the hit and, as it turned out, Bill K has probably benefited from that protection. I could be entirely wrong, but that midday hour, I knew I could kiss goodbye to any thought of ever becoming editor in chief of *Adventist Review* during Paulsen's tenure. Nothing like a spouse offended!

The session behind me, retirement now loomed large, with the date set: Effective Monday, November 1, 2010. And this time, psychologically, I was ready—very ready. The entry in my journal three days before that Monday read, as follows:

*"**10/28/10**. I'd been feeling very upbeat about my upcoming retirement, now just three days away—unlike the dread I experienced sometime last year, when I'd toyed with the idea, sending notice to Paulsen and Bill K, then backing away. Now, when I see copies of announcements going out for yet another cover committee, yet another art conference, I feel a sense of profound relief that I don't have to mess with these any more. I feel as if emerging from under a heavy burden.*

Yet I've enjoyed my time at AR/AW—the privileges and opportunities it afforded me. I did find it somewhat confining and restricting, however, often getting the impression that I was not learning much as I busied myself with editing, scheduling, manuscript evaluation, art conferencing, cover planning, etc. It all seemed to rob me of sufficient time for serious Bible study, reading, and meditation. And as I think that now, at last, I'll be free to do these things, a glow would come over me.

I have a worry, however, that some bubble will burst some time, and that mornings will come when I'd wish I could be going to the office. Will that really happen? My position at the GC often thrust me into the limelight. Will I now be able to stand being in the shadows? Will I miss the attention? Will I miss the daily association with colleagues—in my office and throughout the complex? I can't know that now. But I brace myself."

And, finally, my journal entry the first day of retirement— one of complete relief:

"Today is November 1, 2010, the first day of the rest of my life.

My retirement begins today! Yesterday I finished clearing my office; so that this morning there shouldn't be anything in there pertaining to me. I awoke naturally [after sleeping in the guest room]. The bedroom door was open, meaning that my wife had already left for work. [Since it was still dark,]I rolled over in bed, thinking to go back to sleep. About 5 minutes later, when sleep wouldn't come, I sneaked a peek at the clock. 7:05! I'd slept about 8 hours, in contrast to the 6 ½ I would get when I was working. Not bad. And I can go back to bed later if I feel like it!

*My feeling this morning—though I have no idea how long it would last—is one of complete relief; as if a burden has been removed. No cover committees, no art conferences, no scheduling meetings, no endless evaluation of manuscripts. Now everything I read will be what I **want** to read. Wow!"*

It's now 2014 as I write this last paragraph of the current chapter; and there hasn't been a single day so far when I've wished that I were at the office. Not one! Yes, there's life after retirement, after all.

CHAPTER **18**

Through It All—God's Sustaining Promises

CLOSE TO 40 years ago, I heard former General Conference (GC) president Neal C Wilson make a statement I've never forgotten. "At the beginning of every day," he said, "I pray for two things: *wisdom and courage.*" It was an autobiographical disclosure, giving me an insight into his life; letting me in on what he considered a key coping mechanism in his work.

Every time I hear such real-life testimonies, I'm listening. I'm listening to pick up not many things, necessarily, but often just one thing that I can put into practice in my own situation. And in this chapter, as I bring this memoir to a close, I want to share, for what it's worth, four promises in the Bible that have encouraged and kept me through the decades. Promises I've turned to most frequently—for strength, for wisdom, for encouragement, for help in the dark times. The first two I will deal with only briefly, the last two at greater length.

The first promise is **John 15:4, 5:** "Remain in me, and I will remain in you. No branch can bear fruit by itself; it must remain in the vine. Neither can you bear fruit unless you remain in me. I am the vine; you are the branches. If a man remains in me and I in him, he will bear much fruit; apart from me you can do nothing."

As I would get to my office in the morning, I very frequently would open my Bible to that passage in John 15. For me, it lies at the foundation of the Christian life. A primary slogan of the 2008 Barak

Obama presidential campaign was: "Yes, we can!" And often at the beginning of a rally—and sometimes in the middle of his speech—the audience would spontaneously break out into a chant of the slogan— "Yes, we can! Yes, we can!" But what's OK as a political campaign slogan would be totally inappropriate for the Christian life. For here the appropriate refrain is not "Yes, we can," but "No, we can't!"

That's what Jesus is saying in the passage before us: "Apart from me you can do nothing."

One of our big temptations today is our dependence on gadgets and technology for the prosecution of the task before us. We should not despise technology and other modern equipment in our work. I for one wish I knew everything there is to know about technology. I wish I knew how to operate every machine, every gadget, every program out there. But if I did, I would still be in desperate need when it comes to the spiritual realities of life. That was the essence of Jesus' remarks 2000 years ago: "Remain in me; and I will remain in you," for "apart from me you can do nothing."

So every hectic, working day, as I faced the never-ending deadlines of an editorial office trying to produce a weekly multi-page magazine, I would pause to recognize that, in the end, it all comes about through God's enabling power. Without Him, I can do nothing! He must abide in me and I in Him.

It is true, especially in our technological age, that we can seem to accomplish a great deal on our own; by our own power and ingenuity. But those would be ordinary things, human things, not the things of the Spirit. Spiritual things lie on an entirely different plane, a dimension beyond our native human skill. And it's to those realities that Jesus' words refer: "apart from me you can do nothing."

I felt my need of Him every morning.

The *second promise* is **James 1:5.** "If any of you lacks wisdom, you should ask God, who gives generously to all without finding fault, and it will be given to you."

One definition of wisdom—my own—is *the ability to know what to do; when to do it; and how.* Wisdom is different from knowledge.

Knowledge has to do with information, as such. Wisdom takes that information and helps us act in a way that achieves the best outcome under the circumstances.

As I joined the *Adventist Review* as an editor, I keenly sensed my need for this heavenly ability, and expressed it in the first editorial that I wrote. While struggling to avoid grammatical errors and typos, I indicated, "the greater vigilance should be in avoiding errors of ... theology, errors of doctrine, errors of judgment." "This calls for wisdom," I said. "To know when to speak and when not to. What to say and what not to. How to say it and how not to. Which issues to cover and which to leave alone. I crave this rare discernment and sagacity." (See "A Prayer as I Begin," *Adventist Review*, Dec. 1, 1988, p. 5; reprinted in Adams, *From the Heart* (Alma Park, Grantham,Lincs: Stanborough Press, 2007), p. 12.)

Wisdom helps us size up a situation, and guides us on how to relate to it appropriately and effectively. It's an attainment, an ability, that cannot be hurried. I felt the need for it every day. And it is a quality I leaned on heavily in 2006, the very year (as already explained) when I was facing some of the most unsettling issues of my career.

Years earlier, I'd agreed to prepare the Sabbath School lessons for the second quarter of 2008, with a manuscript deadline of 2006. The author of those lessons is usually asked to prepare a companion book to accompany the studies, and I also had agreed to do that. The deadline would be January 2007. Meanwhile, Stanborough Press in England called and asked whether I would be willing to pull together some of the editorials I'd written over the years for publication in book form. Thinking that that would be a breeze (since the pieces were already written), I agreed. Thus 2006 found me working on three book manuscripts at the same time.

And I discovered that I'd grossly underestimated the difficulty and complexity of putting those editorials together. First, I had to re-read a whole host of them in order to make the initial selection. Then for the second cut, I had to select the ones that contained no time-sensitive elements. Next, I had to find a way of downloading the published piece from our internet archives and deal with the formatting nightmare involved. Finally, each selection had to be updated and reedited for the new setting (for example, an expression like "five months ago" in the original editorial would be inappropriate in the new format). It was exhausting work!

And all this came on top of the unrelenting deadlines of a publication office! An incredible and frightening undertaking, when I look back on it now. Two or three times that year I came close to panicking, with nightmares that I wouldn't be able to pull it off.

That's when I fled to God for wisdom. Wisdom to know how to handle and organize each waking hour at my disposal; wisdom to know how to balance my office work with these extracurricular items on my plate; wisdom to know how, at the same time, to take care of family responsibilities and relationships. So I would pray for wisdom—especially on those days when I hadn't a clue what I was doing; or where I was headed; or even where I needed to go.

Wisdom. I pled with God for it every day. And I was always encouraged by the promise in the text that it was God's will to endue me with it, if I asked.

The *third promise* is **Psalm 20:1, 2:** *"The Lord hear thee in the day of trouble; the name of the God of Jacob defend thee; send thee help from the sanctuary, and strengthen thee out of Zion"* (KJV).

As I've already indicated in this memoir, this is a promise I turn to in moments of deep frustration and in times of crisis. Those times when, for one reason or another, I feel entirely helpless.

At home I have a little office, only 140 sq. ft. (about 13 sq. meters) in size. But I've been surprised again and again at how totally lost things can get in that little place. I would find myself, for example, searching for a document I had in my hand just a week or two earlier, a document that could not leave the room on its own, but which now I cannot find anywhere. And it's *urgent* that I do.

Many times, after spending several futile hours searching down that little room, getting more frustrated every minute, I'd suddenly remember the promise of this passage. In the midst of my frustration, I'd stop; repeat the promise of the passage before the Lord, so to speak; pause in silence before Him; then resume the search. And again and again, I've seen the document turn up within minutes following my prayer—sometimes in a corner of my desk that I'd already turned upside down three times; sometimes under some magazine; sometimes misfiled in some folder that the Lord brings to my attention. That has been my experience.

Then there are times when bigger issues have been at stake—as in the following example.

For months, my wife and I had been planning a trip to Spain and Portugal; and now, finally, we were ready—or so we thought. Sunday evening would be our flight. But it's Friday evening now, and I'm in my study preparing to teach a Sabbath School class at my local church in the morning.

Suddenly, the up-coming trip pops into mind, and something like a voice inside me says: "Check your passports." I stop my preparation, open the drawer on my study desk, and check my own passport first. It's good. Then I turn to my wife's, and in a split second the whole world turns upside down. It's expired.

Crisis.

Tickets have been bought; hotels in both Spain and Portugal booked with credit card—the money non-refundable; and all other arrangements have been made. I sat at my desk stunned. What *are* we going to do? How does one solve a problem like that?

I breathed a prayer, invoking the promise of Psalm 20:1, 2. Then exiting my office, I break the disturbing news to my wife. In a state of near panic, I managed to track down one of the persons from the GC who handles visa and passport renewals. The earliest they could help me, he said, was the following Monday, and they couldn't promise to get it all done in one day either. "Why not change your flight time to next Tuesday or Wednesday?" he said, unwittingly betraying his unfamiliarity with modern air travel. (You don't just call the airlines these days and say: "Sorry, but we can't travel Sunday anymore. Put us on a flight leaving Tuesday or Wednesday." That doesn't happen anymore, if it ever did. Today the slightest change in schedule comes with huge, obscene costs. Besides, all kinds of work arrangements—for both of us—would be disrupted; there'd be conflicts in upcoming appointments; and hotel and other reservations would be in jeopardy.

Desperate, we turn to the yellow pages (the year was 2003, and people still consulted that ancient source). Celia goes to the Federal Government pages and lands upon a number for a government passport office, offering special week-end services. But there was a catch: the services were for diplomats, US government officials, and members of Congress.

The last we checked, we didn't fall in any of the three categories. But we dialed the number anyway.

Now remember this is a Friday night—it's the weekend. In the best of times, you don't expect to find a living, breathing person when you call a government office, but that evening—and it had to be nothing short of divine Providence—-we not only managed to connect to a human being working after hours, but that person just happened to be pleasant, helpful, and kind (a rare phenomenon in the typical government agency today). The agent explained to us what we needed to do, what documents to bring; and that this special office that regularly serves diplomats, State Department officials, and Congress people, would make an exception for us! We must be there at 9:00 a.m. Saturday morning.

And as for my Sabbath school class, again something unusual happened. I phoned Larry Evans, one of my colleagues at the GC office. I reached him (and not his answering machine), and he agreed to take my class.

To shorten the story, we appeared at the government office Sabbath morning (it was an ox-in-the-pit situation, I hope you understand), and in less than three hours (would have been much shorter if their computers had not broken down), we had the new passport in our hands, ready to travel the following day.

Whose voice was it that spoke to me Friday night? Can you think of the nightmare it would have been for us to arrive at the airline check-in counter Sunday evening with an expired passport?

The God of Jacob had come through for us.

The *fourth promise* comes from **Isaiah 40:29-31**: "He gives power to the weak, and to those who have no might He increases strength. Even the youths shall faint and be weary, and the young men shall utterly fall, but those who wait on the Lord shall renew their strength; they shall mount up with wings like eagles, they shall run and not be weary, they shall walk and not faint" (NKJV).

I have turned to this promise in times of high stress; in times when my energy level is almost at zero; in times when I feel the need for critical strength I do not have.

One such instance occurred in connection with a trip I made to the south Pacific in June 2004, and about which I wrote in an editorial in the *Adventist Review* for September 9, 2004. (In the next several paragraphs, I borrow from that piece.)

In the spring of 2003, (then) South Pacific Division (SPD) president Laurie Evans approached me with the request to keynote (and otherwise participate in) a Ministers Summit in Papua New Guinea (PNG) and Fiji, beginning Tuesday evening, June 15, 2004—more than a year away. Though we sometimes can't anticipate how busy we'd be a year out, that time I did. I knew I'd be climbing the walls come that date, and it was an invitation I didn't want to accept. But Evans probably caught me in a weak moment, and I agreed. As the time got closer, I booked a flight to leave Washington Saturday evening, June 12, to arrive in PNG sometime Monday 14, giving me about a day or so to rest up and do my final preparations.

But even if I'd managed to predict how crazy my schedule would be around the time of the appointment, I could not anticipate that the situation would be complicated even further by the passing of my mother-in-law on the very eve of the trip.

Mom had been ailing for more than a year; and for the final four months of that time, it had been touch and go on a weekly, even a daily, basis. At one point Celia, thinking her mom was in the final throes, had traveled to Orlando where she lived, only to return to Maryland with her mom still fighting. She was a strong woman.

Finally, however, she succumbed—in the early hours of June 10, two days before I was due to leave. Her funeral would be on Sunday, June 13 at high noon.

Frantically, I called the airline to reschedule my flight to PNG, and sent word to the SPD about my new itinerary. So the time that would normally have gone into breakneck, last-minute sermon preparation for the summit now found me busily brushing up on a funeral message, since my mother-in-law's pastor had begged off for some crazy reason I don't even want to remember now.

Thus, instead of heading out for Sydney en route to Papua New Guinea Saturday night, June 12, I was traveling instead to Orlando to join my wife who'd gone ahead. I was still preparing my funeral message before rolling into bed late Saturday night. Sunday afternoon, the burial and family visiting over, I headed back to the airport for a circuitous return flight to Washington.

Arriving home at 1:00 a.m. Monday morning, I immediately commenced the complicated business of packing for the extended trip to the South Pacific, finishing about 2:30 a.m. After a quick shower, I hit the sack at about 2:45, asking our daughter Kim (who'd picked me up earlier that night) to give me a wake-up call at 4:30, and be ready to take me back to the airport.

I was a basket case as I left home in the wee hours that Monday morning, surviving on adrenaline—no stimulants of any kind would ever pass my lips. I would fly first to Sydney (Australia), then to Port Moresby (PNG's capital), then on to Lae, the country's second largest city. From there, a two-hour ride would take me to the site of the meetings. Forty-four hours after leaving Washington, I arrived at my destination, with my keynote message less than four hours away.

Scary memories flooded my mind in the anxious hours before that first meeting—memories about how exhausted I'd feel when speaking at evening meetings in Los Angeles or Seattle or Vancouver (Canada), after all-day flights from the east coast of the U.S., only three time zones away. Memories about dozing off for split seconds in the midst of lectures at our seminary near Manila in the Philippines—from jet lag, after returning from furloughs in the U.S. So what would happen now, facing as I did the mother of all jet-lags?

That evening I spoke without feeling a single sniff of tiredness or fatigue. It was as though strong, invisible arms had come to my support. I felt fresh, lucid, alert. At the funeral, I'd earnestly asked the congregation to pray for me. "Call my name," I begged them; and they promised. Now God had come through for me. Recognizing my utter helplessness, I'd leaned the heaviest I could remember on His promise through Isaiah: "He gives power to the weak, and to those who have no might He increases strength."

It turned out to be an enjoyable trip, and one filled with fellowship. GC colleagues Jim and Sharon Cress were present at the summit, and so too was retired GC ministerial associate director, Joel Sarli. During the meetings themselves, I hardly saw them, their presentations coming during the daytime, while mine took place in the evening. But we were all together as we traveled from Lae to overnight in Port Moresby, before flying on to Nadi (or Nandi) in Western Fiji, en route to Suva (on the southeastern end of Fiji's main island), site of the next meetings. Also with us were (then) SPD ministerial director Anthony Kent (our host) and (for part of the way) his wife Debora. The swapping of stories that went on, the bantering, the practical jokes, the testimonies, the reflections—what good fellowship!

But the PNG stint left on me a lasting impression. The Lord not only sustained me throughout, but also inspired me with examples of dedication, sacrifice, and the power of grace. As we sat on the rostrum together one evening, I asked one of our pastors how far he'd come to attend the meetings. "Three days by boat," he said. And suddenly, my 44 hours by plane seemed minor. There were chairs in the (open-sided) structure where we met, but not enough for all 700 attendees. So dozens of pastors and their spouses sat on the concrete floor—on mats, blankets, whatever. Yet they stayed with the meetings from early morning till past 9:00 in the evening—patient, uncomplaining, attentive.

At the end of my sermon one evening, as a group of pastors and their spouses came forward to sing, I sat behind them reflecting. One hundred years ago, I thought, the ancestors of these people literally ate some of the missionaries who arrived in their villages. Today, the descendants of these cannibals are singing about the power of the cross!

I felt hot tears flow as I saw God's power in the lives of these wonderful sisters and brothers. And I felt His strong hand in my own life.

On countless other occasions over the years I've leaned on that hope-filled promise of Isaiah 40—when there was some disagreeable assignment I had to do; some unpleasant task I had to perform; some difficult person I needed to encounter; some issue I had to face. I've clung to it in times when I'd fallen flat on my face, feeling I just couldn't handle whatever was before me; in times when I'd appeared for some preaching assignment tired, dispirited, unprepared.

That last situation befell me one October night in St. Vincent in 2002.

I'd gone to the Eastern Caribbean Conference to speak on the occasion of a special anniversary for that field. I arrived on a Thursday afternoon, and had my first meeting Friday morning at the conference office—with pastors, teachers, conference staff, and other Adventist workers in attendance. A question and answer session followed; and after lunch, with one or two stops at points of interest, I was quickly whisked back to the hotel to prepare for a heavy Sabbath speaking schedule.

Friday evening I spoke at our Black Rock church; Sabbath morning they took me to another large congregation, the one near the University of the West Indies (Barbados campus); went for lunch at conference president James Daniel's home, visiting all the while with the many students he and his wife Margaret had invited. Later that afternoon, I spoke again at the same church, with an open forum (with difficult and controversial questions) following. Sunday night, I spoke at yet another location on the island, and flew out Monday morning with Daniel, en route to St. Vincent, the second of my four-island itinerary.

From the airport we headed to the harbor in the capital of Kingstown, caught a ferry, and set out for the tiny island of Bequia, off the coast. It took us an unexpectedly long while getting settled in a guesthouse a few miles (or so it felt) from the landing docks, ending up with no supper that evening. After a quick shower, it was off to an evangelistic meeting, whose speaker agreed to stand down that one night so I could bring the sermon.

(I've referred on many occasions to my experience that evening—the song service, in particular. As the people broke out into that old Advent song, "Watch, Ye Saints, with eyelids waking," accompanied by drums, keyboard, saxophone, and other musical instruments, you felt goose bumps beginning to form; and as they went into the chorus, "Lo! He comes, lo! Jesus comes....," you got the impression that if you were to exit the tent and look toward the eastern skies, you'd actually see the Lord returning.)

Tuesday morning, after a quick breakfast, we headed back to St. Vincent, where Daniel had arranged a meeting with the country's prime minister, followed by lunch with the PM's senior assistant, Louis Straker, who happened to be a Seventh-day Adventist. That evening, I spoke at one of our local churches, and Wednesday morning took a meeting with all our pastors and some of our other workers on the island.

This means that I'd been going almost non-stop for five days. And that Wednesday evening, as we headed far out into the countryside for another service, I was tired—very tired. As the car made its way through the narrow, winding, hilly roads to the place, I sat at the back of the vehicle, trying to collect my thoughts between dozes.

As the service got underway, a group of young people came forward and sang "a special" out of the *Adventist Church Hymnal*. (For reasons I don't myself understand, I always find it a tad off-putting when members fall back on the church hymnal for the special music. It seems to lack a certain *je ne sais quoi*—a certain something I cannot define. Frankly, it did not lift my spirits.)

That done, I sat there listening to President Daniel introducing me as some big-time speaker from the GC! And I'm thinking: *If he only knew!*

"Lord," I prayed under my breath, "how can I preach here tonight? I feel as if I have nothing compelling to say! I'm so utterly tired and dispirited."

His introduction complete, Daniel spoke an unexpected sentence, since I thought the special music was already behind us. "Before Dr. Adams speaks, I understand that Brother Anderson will present a special song."

About a year or so earlier, I'd been speaking at a pastors' conference in New Zealand's North Island, near Rotorua; and as I drove back and forth to the meetings each day, I managed to lock onto a religious radio station, where I ran into a song by Ray Boltz that simply blew me away. Determined to not leave the country without it, I tracked down the cassette (yes, cassette—remember those?), not knowing that I could easily have picked it up in the U.S. I was captivated by the simple message of the piece; it inspired me; and I played it over and over.

In God's marvelous timing and providence, that was the song Brother Anderson chose to sing that evening:

I have journeyed through the long, dark night,
Out on the open sea;
By faith alone, sight unknown,
And Yet His eyes were watching me.

The anchor holds, though the ship is battered.
The anchor holds, though the sails are torn.
I have fallen on my knees
As I faced the raging seas.
The anchor holds, in spite of the storm.*

Brother Anderson sang with passion and deep feeling, in my

opinion almost better than Boltz himself. And, mysteriously, God used those words and that music to lift me out of my emotional quagmire, enabling me to bring a message of encouragement and hope to those who'd gathered. I left the place feeling light and joyful and utterly grateful for the way God comes through for me when I feel absolutely weak and dispirited.

"They that wait upon the Lord shall renew their strength."

THE ANCHOR HOLDS, Ray Boltz/Larence Chewning;© 1994 Shepherd Boy Music (Admin. by Word Music, LLC), Word Music, LLC, All Rights Reserved. Used by Permission. If the site is still active, check out my favorite recording of the song at https://www.youtube.com/watch?v=vL_BnW1LAg0

Postscript

As I look back across the decades, I find abundant evidence of God's hand in my life. He took this dirt-poor, shirt-tailed Anglican boy from one of the tiniest inhabited islands on earth, placed him at the headquarters of the global Seventh-day Adventist Church, and sent him on missions all around the world. It is sheer, unadulterated grace. And notwithstanding all the vicissitudes I've encountered, I've never once experienced a loss of confidence in God. He has been "a shelter for me, and a *strong tower* from the enemy" (Ps. 61:3, KJV).

But the past is past. The unknown future lies ahead. And for anyone over 60, the realization eventually sinks in that the bulk of one's years lies behind them. That however much the Lord protects, however much God renews our strength, our general vitality continues on a downward path, the inevitable aging process taking its toll. It's the human condition; and no amount of rejuvenation prescriptions, programs, or pep talks can permanently hold it back. As we see members of the previous generation pass off the stage one by one, we get an eerie sense that our turn is coming.

As the apostle Paul confronted this inexorable human situation, he pointed to a future that absolutely transcends it: "For we know that if our earthly house, this tent, is destroyed, we have a building from God, a house not made with hands, eternal in the heavens" (2 Cor. 5:1, NKJV). And John, the nonagenarian exile of Patmos, his own mortality staring him in the face, painted a picture for the encouragement of Christians down the centuries: "Now I saw a new heaven and a new earth, for the first heaven and the first earth had passed away. Also there was no more sea. Then I, John, saw the holy city, New Jerusalem, coming down out of heaven from God, prepared as a bride adorned for her husband. And I heard a loud voice from heaven saying, 'Behold, the tabernacle of God *is* with men, and He will dwell with them, and they shall be His people. God Himself will be with them and be their God. And God will wipe away every tear from their eyes; there shall be no more death, nor sorrow, nor crying. There shall be no more pain, for the former things have passed away'" (Rev. 21:1-4, NKJV).

Those words of Scripture, a defiant commentary on the obscenity of aging, sickness, and death, perk me up every time I read them, giving me a glance at the big picture, a sneak preview of how the human drama ends. They've fed the hunger for certainty across the centuries, inspiring some of the most moving sentiments in literature and music—whether elaborate oratorios or simple gospels—as in in the case of Maryland native Charles Tindley. Familiar with hardship, privation, and even slavery (his father was a slave), Tindley pinned his hope on a future beyond the things of time, writing and setting to music words that have inspired millions since they were written more than a hundred years ago:

Beams of heaven, as I go
Through this wilderness below,
Guide my feet in peaceful ways,
Turn my midnights into days.
When in the darkness I would grope,
Faith always sees a star of hope,
And soon from all life's grief and danger
I shall be free someday.
I do not know how long 'twill be,
Nor what the future holds for me,
But this I know: if Jesus leads me,
I shall get home someday.

To listen to a musical rendition of those words by a competent soloist or choir would tingle the spine of every Christian. I found myself hardly able to keep my seat as twice in one day this past April I heard them performed by the Oakwood Aeolians under the direction of Jason Max Ferdinand, in an arrangement whose goose-pimple finale stirred the deepest emotions of the soul with an ardent yearning for that celestial country to which Tindley looked forward with such resilient hope. That same hope captures my imagination ever more powerfully with every passing day.

Mine has not been a triumphalist ministry. I've always been keenly aware of my inadequacies, my ignorance, my many foibles and weaknesses; and my life has seen its fair share of twists and turns, ups and downs, zigzags and back-pedaling. Even now, not a single day goes by but that I sense the deepest need of God's inscrutable grace. Every day I fall back on the promise in the words of the ancient prophet: *"The name of the Lord is a strong tower; the righteous run to it and are safe"* (Prov. 18:10). And every day the sentiments of my prayer echo that of the psalmist: "O send out your light and your truth; let them lead me; let them bring me to your holy hill and to your dwelling" (Psa. 43:3, NRSV).

Yes, God has been my Rock of Gibraltar, my strong tower, my unfailing beacon in the night. Throughout my ministry I have sensed those strong, invisible beams of light leading me, guiding me, protecting me. And in the darkest periods of my life I could say, in the sentiments of Psalm 27:1—

"The Lord is my light and my salvation—
whom shall I fear?
The Lord is the stronghold of my life—
of whom shall I be afraid?"